COAST TO COAST

WORKBOOK 3

Jeremy Harmer, Karen Davy,
and Steve Elsworth

Longman

London and New York

Longman Group UK Limited,
Longman House, Burnt Mill, Harlow,
Essex CM20 2JE, England
and Associated Companies throughout the world.

Published in the United States of America
by Longman Inc., The Longman Building,
95 Church Street, White Plains,
NY 10601, U.S.A.

First published 1988

Set in 10/12 pt Univers medium

Printed in Great Britain
by Butler & Tanner Ltd., Frome & London

ISBN 0-582-90736-5

Illustrated by George Parkin and Gaye Galsworthy

New vocabulary and expressions

Vocabulary items marked * first occur in the *Interaction* or *Listening* sections of the Student's Book, or in the Workbook. Nouns are marked (n) to indicate usage in the text where confusion is possible.

Geographic features
bayou
canyon*
delta
forest
gulf
ocean*
oil well

Jobs
employment agency*
job hunting*
job seeker*
promotion*

New Orleans / Mardi Gras
Cajun
float (n)
French Quarter
mask
parade (n)

Sports equipment
hang glider
high wire
surfboard
unicycle

Travel
airline*
arrangements*

guide (n)*
international*
representative (rep)*

Various
army
bathtub
beer
captain
celebrity*
character
club (n)
confusing*
to depend
(to get) desperate
dramatic
to drill

enchilada*
enjoyable*
exam*
exhausted
exhausting*
exit (n)
feature* (n)
fictional
figure (n)
fire drill
forecast (n)*
giant-sized
governor
guacamole*
hood*
medical bill

medicine*
mural
to own
product*
puzzled*
to row
sidewalk*
soldier*
star (n)*
(to be a) success
tape (n)*
task*
thunderstorm
unusual
warm*
well-known
to wonder

---

1 Vocabulary

Circle the word or expression that is different from the others.

1 coast (forest) beach ocean

2 president governor mayor soldier

3 thunderstorm traffic jam hurricane earthquake

4 beer taco enchilada guacamole

5 recipe menu ingredient exam

6 mountain desert wind canyon

---

2 Review: *-ed* and *-ing* participles

Complete this advertisement by writing the appropriate adjective in each of the blanks. Choose either the *-ed* or *-ing* participle listed in the box on the right.

JOB SEEKERS INTERNATIONAL

Are you [1] *bored* .... at your job? Do you do the same

[2] .... things all day long? If you are looking for

[3] .... work, we are sure that you will find this ad

[4] .... We know how [5] .... it is to go

from employment agency to employment agency. Job seekers are often

[6] .... and [7] .... by the end of their first

week of job hunting! JOB SEEKERS INTERNATIONAL can help with this

[8] .... task. Call us today at 924-3800.

1	bored/boring
2	bored/boring
3	excited/exciting
4	interested/interesting
5	exhausted/exhausting
6	exhausted/exhausting
7	confused/confusing
8	confused/confusing

3 Review: simple past, past continuous, present perfect

Choose the correct verb form and write it in the blank.

I left the house and 1 *walked* .... to my car. I 2 .... my keys when I
                walked/was walking   was looking for/looked for

3 .... a strange noise. The noise 4 .... from under the hood. I was very puzzled
    heard/have heard   was coming/has come

because I 5 .... my car for two years without any problems so far. Anyway, I finally
            have had/had

6 .... my keys. When I 7 .... the hood, I couldn't believe my eyes! A cat
    have found/found   have opened/opened

8 .... on the engine. I 9 .... the cat and put it on the sidewalk. Since then,
    was sitting/has sat   was picking up/picked up

I 10 .... under the hood before I start the car.
    have always checked/always checked

4 Review: joining sentences

Rewrite these pairs of sentences, joining them with *although* or *because*.

1 Our neighbors want to move. Their apartment is too small. *Our neighbors want to move*
because their apartment is too small.

2 They might have to move to the suburbs. They love their neighborhood here in the city. ....

3 They're thinking about buying a house. They have two small children. ....

4 They will probably find a house they can afford. Houses are cheaper in the suburbs. ....

5 I know they will be happy in the suburbs. I will miss them. ....

Now join these pairs of sentences using *so* or *because*.

6 I've just gotten a big promotion. I'm going to have a party. ....

7 I've invited my boss and his wife. I want my husband to meet them. ....

8 I had to clean the house for the party. I didn't go to work today. ....

5 Writing

Read the computer printout about Mr. and Mrs. Monroe's
Mexican vacation. Then read the letter that the travel agent
sent them.

```
NAME -- MR. & MRS. P. MONROE -- MEXICO CITY
                          (Hotel Presidente)

Flight number and date
Departure time from Dulles      MEX 66, May 23
   International Airport
Arrival time at Benito          9:20 A.M.
   Juárez Airport
Hotel rep at airport?           2:00 P.M.
Drive to hotel                  Yes
Name of tour guide              45 mins. to 1 hr.
Starting date of tour           Ms. Lupe Moreno
Weather forecast                May 25
                                warm & sunny
```

Dear Mr. and Mrs. Monroe:

I am glad to be able to confirm the arrangements for your trip to Mexico City. You are flying on flight MEX 66, which will leave Dulles International Airport on May 23 at 9:20 A.M. and arrive at Benito Juárez Airport at 2:00 P.M. There will be a representative from your hotel, Hotel Presidente; he or she will drive you to the hotel, a ride that will take between 45 minutes and one hour.

Your tour guide is Lupe Moreno, and your tour starts on May 25. Ms. Moreno is going to contact you at your hotel on May 24.

The weather in Mexico City at the end of May will be warm and sunny. I wish you a pleasant trip and a very enjoyable vacation.

Sincerely yours,

Pat d'Amici

Now read the travel details for Mr.
Lento and write the travel agent's
letter to him.

```
NAME -- MR. FRANK LENTO -- SAN JUAN
                          (Hotel Don Pedro)

Flight number and date          AA 699, February 3
Departure time from Kennedy
   International Airport         8:00 A.M.
Arrival time at San Juan
   International Airport         11:38 A.M.
Hotel rep at airport?           No (take a taxi)
Drive to hotel                  10-20 mins.
Name of tour guide              Larry Murphy
Starting date of tour           February 5
Weather forecast                hot & sunny
```

New vocabulary and expressions

Vocabulary items marked * first occur in the *Interaction* or *Listening* sections of the Student's Book, or in the Workbook. Nouns are marked (n) to indicate usage in the text where confusion is possible.

The mind
mental breakdown*
optimistic
to overreact*
pessimistic
tension*

Radio
drama series
pop music
quiz program
selection
station

Exercise
bicycle (n)
to burn calories
to keep in shape
to stay fit

Surveys
a half
percent
results
three-quarters

Various
activity*
to agree
animation techniques*
appetite*
to babysit (for)*
to blame
cartoons*
classmate*
clothes*
collection
column
customer

especially
extensive
to fall asleep
guy
idea
to invest
lightbulb*
orally*
to organize
outdoors*
overseas
pearls
politics*

quality
(to keep a) secret*
(to sleep) soundly
special
topic
whole
in writing*

1 What's the verb?

Find a verb in the following list that can be used with both of the words or phrases. You will use each verb only once.

| keep   change   lose   switch   check   burn |

1 *burn* .... energy/calories

2 .... weight/your appetite

3 .... a 50-dollar bill/a lightbulb

4 .... in shape/a secret

5 .... the oil/the tires

6 .... stations/channels

2 Verbs + -ing

Write new sentences by adding the verb in parentheses.

1 Marcia is happy here. (work) *Marcia is happy working here.*

2 Many young women are not interested in children. (babysit for) ....

3 But Marcia has always enjoyed children. (take care of) ....

4 All of Marcia's children love pizza. (eat) ....

5 Most parents can't stand children's television programs. (listen to) ....

6 But Marcia likes cartoons. (watch) ....

7 She is very interested in the new animation techniques. (study) ....

3 Likes and dislikes

Do you like or dislike these things? Write *L* or *D* in the boxes.

1 taking a cold shower ☐
2 visiting relatives ☐
3 eating in restaurants ☐
4 talking about politics ☐
5 wearing old clothes ☐

6 staying up all night ☐
7 camping ☐
8 watching baseball games ☐
9 walking in the rain ☐
10 going to the dentist ☐

Now write a sentence about six of the activities above, using each of these expressions: *like, be interested in, really enjoy; don't like, can't stand, hate.*

1 ....
2 ....
3 ....
4 ....
5 ....
6 ....

4 Expressing preferences

Write about your preferences by answering these questions. Give reasons for your answers.

1 Would you rather travel by plane or by train? *I would rather travel by plane because traveling by plane is faster and more interesting than traveling by train.*

2 Would you rather live in the city or in the country? ....
....
....

3 Would you rather watch your favorite sport or play it? ....
....
....

4 Would you rather answer these questions orally or in writing? ....
....
....

5 Would you rather work in an office or outdoors? ....
....
....

5 Percentages

Look at the results of Radio WQMX's survey on page 10 of *Coast to Coast*
Student's Book 3. Use the information and the code below to complete the bar
graph. (A bar graph is used to show how numbers compare in size.)

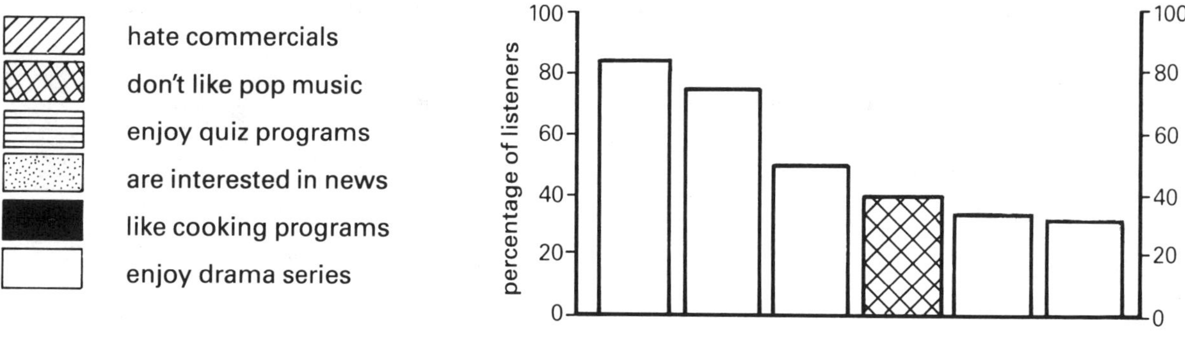

6 Writing

The same survey was organized by WSBR, Radio WQMX's sister station in
Baton Rouge. The results were quite different. Use this graph to write the
second half of the report on page 10 of Student's Book 3, summarizing the
results of WSBR's survey.

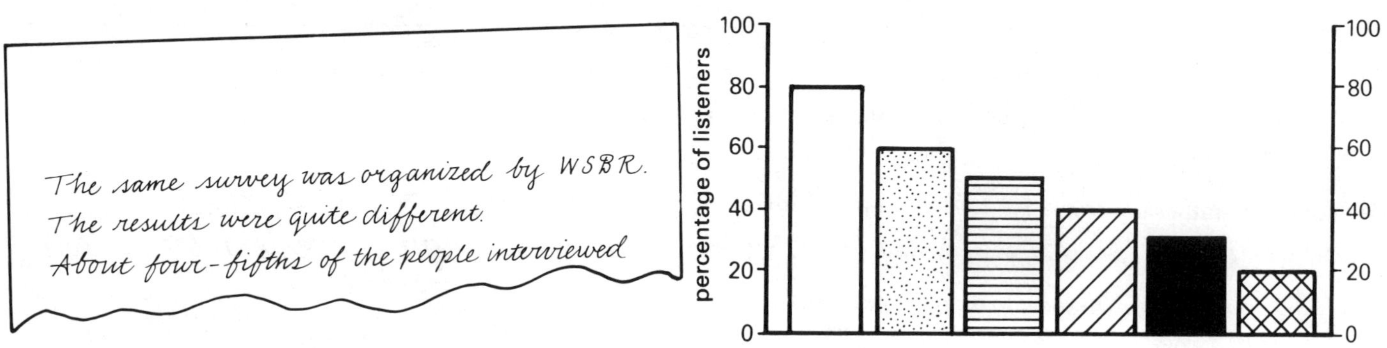

3

1 Vocabulary

Rewrite these sentences, substituting a synonym from the vocabulary box
above for each of the underlined expressions. Note that the meaning of the
sentences should not change.

1 What <u>are you doing</u> these days? *What are you up to these days ?* ....

2 <u>Getting used to</u> a new school is difficult, isn't it? ....

....

3 I always have to <u>make a great effort</u> to get used to new classes. ....

....

4 Someone told me that you weren't using <u>old-fashioned</u> methods anymore. ....

....

5 Do you still tell your students that they are not <u>permitted</u> to speak their own language in your class? ....

....

6 I am very glad that you haven't <u>stopped</u> teaching; you are a wonderful teacher. ....

....

....

2 Safety rules

Read each of the sentences from the Drain Wizard label and decide if it is stating something that is obligatory (O), prohibited (P), desirable (D), or undesirable (U).

DRAIN WIZARD

1 Important: Read the entire label before using this product. ..O....

2 If possible, remove the drain strainer. ....

3 Never use Drain Wizard when the water in the drain is hot. ....

4 We recommend that you run cold water for at least 5 minutes before introducing Drain Wizard. ....

5 Keep the container away from the face while opening and pouring. ....

6 Try not to breathe while pouring Drain Wizard into the drain. ....

7 Try to avoid contact with skin and clothing. ....

8 Do not take Drain Wizard internally. ....

9 Always keep this can out of children's reach. ....

10 If you have any questions about this product, please call 1-800-362-8416. ....

3 Expressing obligation and desirability

The manufacturers of Drain Wizard want to revise, or change, the instructions on their label. Rewrite each of the sentences in Exercise 2, using *must/must not* and *should/should not*.

1 *You must read the entire label before using this product.*

2 ....

3 ....

4 ....

5 ....

6 ....

7 ....

8 ....

9 ....

10 ....

4 Writing

Read this letter to Allie, the writer of an advice column that appears in newspapers all over the country.

Dear Allie,

I am writing to you because I just do not know what to do. My boyfriend is 21 and I am 20; we have been together for five years. When we were in high school, we went to parties and movies every weekend. But since we left school, he never wants to go anywhere. All he wants to do on Friday and Saturday nights is sit in the living room with my parents and watch TV. (Sometimes I don't even see him on Friday.) We both have jobs, so the problem is not money. What should I do?

Bored in Birmingham

Now write Allie's response to "Bored," making suggestions and giving advice. Begin as follows:

Dear Bored,
I agree that you have a problem. I think you should

New vocabulary and expressions

Vocabulary items marked * first occur in the *Interaction* or *Listening* sections of the Student's Book, or in the Workbook. Nouns are marked (n) to indicate usage in the text where confusion is possible.

Food/drink	*Regular verbs*	*Various*		
corn	to behave*	afraid	gramophone	rail
goulash*	to bicycle	band	grandfather	science-fiction*
soft drink	to earn*	to be born	to grow (grown)	showboat
	to exist	bed	invasion*	somehow
Occupations	to file	to bet (bet)*	laundry	steamboat
congressman/woman*	to laugh	certainly	ma'am (madam)	step (n)
consultant*	to mind	decision	memory	still*
physician*	to obey*	(to make an) effort	method	though
social worker*	to protest	everywhere	outdated	to understand
waitress*	to refuse	except	outer space*	(understood)
	to request	explanation	outside	wood(en)
	to skate*	fund (n)*	palace*	wrinkled
	to trap	to get mixed up in	pipe	youth
			policy	

1 Dictionary work: word division

In writing, it is often necessary to divide a word when there is no more space on a line. Most words are divided according to their pronunciation. Look at these examples; note the hyphen (-) that separates the syllables.

a-way   re-turn   tel-e-vi-sion   pret-ty

Divide each of these words into syllables; you may want to refer to the rules in the box.

1 behave *be-have*

2 palace ....

3 exist ....

4 interview ....

5 gramophone ....

6 animals ....

7 boring ....

8 sorry ....

9 trapping ....

10 laughed ....

11 describe ....

12 suggestion ....

Now check your answers with your dictionary. Note that most dictionaries use dots (·) instead of hyphens to separate syllables.

---

1 Never divide a one-syllable word.

2 Never divide a word between two or three consonants pronounced as one: *fath-om* (not *fat-hom*).

3 Never divide a word between two consonants when both consonants are part of the original word: *yell-ing* (not *yel-ling*).

2 *Make* or *do*?

Nobuo, an exchange student from Kobe, is living with the Davis family in Santa Barbara, California. Complete his conversation with Mrs. Davis, using an appropriate form of *make* or *do*. (N = Nobuo, M = Mrs. Davis)

N: May I use the telephone? I have to ...*make*........... a quick call.

M: Sure. Use the phone upstairs. Grandma .... the dishes, and

the kids .... a lot of noise in the living room.

N: Yes, but Joel .... his homework upstairs.

M: I'll bet he (neg.) .... anything important. When I ask him to

.... me a favor, homework is just one of many excuses that

he .... He used it when I asked him to ....

the dishes, and he'll use it when I tell him to .... the laundry

too.

3 *Used to*

Allen returned to his hometown and found that many things were different. The waitress at his favorite restaurant was one of the first people Allen spoke to. Write her responses to Allen's questions.

1 Does Lulu own this restaurant? *Lulu used to own this restaurant, but she doesn't anymore.*

2 Do you serve goulash? ....

....

3 Does the cook bake his own bread? ....

....

4 Does the owner accept checks? ....

....

5 But you do accept credit cards, don't you? ....

....

6 Does that famous actress still eat here often? ....

....

7 Do the local sports teams meet here every Friday night? ....

....

8 Is this still the best restaurant in town? ....

....

4 Writing: filling in a form

CABC, a cable-television company in the United States, is hiring consultants from all over the world. Would you like the job? You will be responsible for recommending programs produced in your country that may be of interest to TV viewers in the States.

Fill in the application form, giving details of all the jobs you have had so far; include volunteer work and part-time jobs as well. Under the section labeled GENERAL, write at least four things that you used to do in school, college, or at work that will help you in your application for this job. If you have no real experience, try to invent something that will interest the company. Start your sentences with *I used to*, *I also used to*, and *Finally*.

CABC

APPLICATION FOR EMPLOYMENT
(Pre-employment questionnaire) (An equal opportunity employer)

PERSONAL INFORMATION

Name ____

                   last   first   middle

Permanent address ____

                 street   city   country

Phone number ___________________________ Are you 18 years or older? ___________________________

EMPLOYMENT INFORMATION

Are you employed now? ___________________ On what date can you start with us? ___________________

Have you ever applied to this company before? ____

May we inquire of your present or past employer(s)? ____

SPECIAL QUESTIONS (Do not answer any of these questions unless the employer has checked it.)

Height _________________ ✓Citizen of U.S.? _____________ ✓If no, citizen of _______________

Weight _________________ Date of birth _______________________

✓ What foreign languages do you speak? _____________________
                         read? _____________________
                         write? _____________________

EMPLOYMENT HISTORY

Company name ___________________________ Position held ___________________________

Dates: from _______________ to _______________ Reason for leaving ___________________________

Company name ___________________________ Position held ___________________________

Dates: from _______________ to _______________ Reason for leaving ___________________________

GENERAL (use a separate sheet of paper)

New vocabulary and expressions

Vocabulary items marked * first occur in the *Interaction* or *Listening* sections of the Student's Book, or in the Workbook. Nouns are marked (n) to indicate usage in the text where confusion is possible.

Adjectives
abundant*
attractive*
haunted
realistic*
regular*

Regular verbs
to beg*
to cause*
to groan
to manufacture*
to persuade
to polish*

to produce*
to repeat*
to stare

Soccer
goalkeeper*
match (n)*
semifinal*
stadium*

Various
answer (n)
aid (n)
aisle*

auditorium*
basement*
charity*
chores*
climate*
cook-out*
culture*
deal (n)
death
doubles partner
drummer*
extract (n)*
flower

furniture*
ghost
human*
information*
to lend, lent
lesson*
marathon*
none
nothing
passage*
pattern*
prize*
region*

rhythm*
robot*
shock (n)
soil (n)*
stomachache
streetcar
tamale
tandem (bicycle)
uncle

---

1 Vocabulary

Find the words in the vocabulary box above that mean the same or almost the same as these.

1 a bicycle built for two *tandem*

2 the lowest part of a house ....

3 a dead person who appears again ....

4 a passage taken from a book ....

5 an organization that helps people ....

6 a 26-mile running race ....

7 to cause to do something by reasoning, arguing, begging ....

8 a regular, repeated pattern of sounds ....

---

2 Scrambled sentences

Caroline has a lot to do today. Put the following words and phrases in order to make the sentences on her list.

1 | a birthday present | buy | Sam |

Buy Sam a birthday present.............

2 | get | a new tie | him |

....

3 | Suzy | for her violin lesson | money | give |

....

....

4 | a check | send | the telephone company |

....

....

5 | a thank-you note | Sam's parents | write |

....

....

6 | show | them | the vacation pictures   **8** | her | bring | milk for her cat

....

7 | take | some flowers | Mrs. Tanaka

....

---

3 Facts and figures

Use the information to write sentences with *so/such a . . . that.*

1 Antarctica: cold climate—few humans live there

Antarctica has such a cold climate that few humans live there.

2 The Sahara Desert: dry—almost nothing grows there

....

3 Brazil: large—it covers almost half of South America

....

4 Europe: rich soil and good rainfall—it produces almost enough food to feed its population

....

....

5 Southern Asia: many people to feed—it is a very poor region

....

6 The U.S. and Canada: abundant natural resources—they make more than 25 percent of the world's manufactured goods

....

....

---

4 Writing

Reporters often describe events in terms of cause and effect. Look at the notes
that a sports announcer took at a World Cup soccer semifinal.

Cause	*Effect*
Soccer is a popular sport in this country.	People have come from everywhere to see the match.
Today is an important day.	Most businesses are closed.
The stadium is crowded.	There are fans standing in the aisles.
The fans are making a lot of noise.	The players cannot hear the coaches' instructions.
The visiting team has a strong goalkeeper.	The home team will not score much.
The home team is fast.	The visiting team will have to play well to win.

Now write the announcer's description of the soccer match. Begin as follows:

Soccer is such a popular sport in this country that people . . .

New vocabulary and expressions

Vocabulary items marked * first occur in the *Interaction* or *Listening* sections of the Student's Book, or in the Workbook. Nouns are marked (n) to indicate usage in the text where confusion is possible.

Historical ruins/sites
ancient
black market
cliff dwellings
to destroy
to flood
foundation
jungle
memorial
to preserve
religious
remains (n)
to steal (stolen)
weapon

In the kitchen
egg-timer
scoop (n)
to serve
spoon
wok

Materials
metal
plastic
stainless steel
stone

Police movies
case*
conflict*
cop*
corrupt*
detective*
to expose*
to solve*
thriller*

Various
above
air pollution
to assemble*
to attack

blade*
common*
critic*
extraordinary*
extremely*
federal
hostile*
intriguing
jockey*
network*
normal
port*
proposal*
to pump*

rapid(ly)*
to revolve*
sack
to shake (shaken)
slogan*
to store*
tower*
to turn down*
urban*
various*
vibration
voter*
warehouse*
weird

---

1 Dictionary work: stress

Most dictionaries show where the stress falls on words with two or more syllables. The stress mark appears at the beginning of the syllable that receives the stress: *pocket* / ˈpɑkɪt / *before* / bɪˈfɔr /

Write these words in the boxes and use ' to mark the stressed syllables.

1 ancient	*'ancient*
2 survive	*sur 'vive*
3 preserve	
4 hostile	
5 thriller	
6 jungle	
7 weapon	
8 destroy	
9 network	
10 remain	

11 religious	
12 ceremony	
13 investigator	
14 extraordinary	
15 archaeologist	

Now check your answers with your English-language dictionary.

---

2 Review: parts of speech

Look again at the fifteen words in Exercise 1 above and identify their part of speech. Write *noun*, *verb*, or *adjective* for each word.

1 *adjective*	6	11 ....
2	7	12 ....
3	8	13 ....
4	9	14 ....
5	10	15 ....

3 Using the passive

Rewrite these sentences in the passive. Make sure to keep them in the same tense.

1 A citizens' group in California is using the slogan "Slow Growth!"

The slogan "Slow Growth!" is being used by a citizens' group in California.

2 Construction has damaged a lot of California's natural beauty.

3 Real-estate developers have built office towers and shopping centers in residential areas.

4 The rapidly growing population is endangering Californians' right to privacy.

5 Overbuilding has affected urban as well as suburban areas.

6 San Francisco voters recently turned down a proposal to build a baseball stadium downtown.

4 Describing processes

Decide the order of procedures and describe each of these processes in one sentence.

1 Tables/sent to the stores/assembled in the factories/painted

Tables are assembled in the factories, painted, and sent to the stores.

2 Oranges/put into bags/checked for quality/picked

3 Fish/transported by truck to the cities/caught/taken to the nearest port

4 Tourists/helped with their luggage/taken by taxi to their hotels/met at the airport by our representatives

5 Milk/picked up from the farms by trucks/put into containers/taken to a central warehouse

6 Water/cleaned/pumped to our houses/taken from the Great Lakes

5 Describing

It is the year 2090 and a historian has found four objects from 1989. Which passage describes each object?

Answer: **1** ...... **2** ...... **3** ...... **4** ......

1 It is made of plastic, glass, and metal, and looks like a box. The important part of this machine is the front, which is made of glass and is square in shape.

When the machine was turned on, pictures could be seen through the glass. The machine was used for home entertainment, and was very popular in the twentieth century.

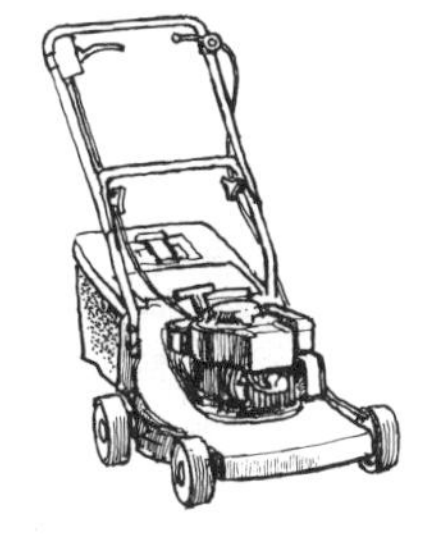

A

2 This strange-looking object was very common in the last century, but has now completely disappeared. It was used for storing information, which was kept on paper at the time. This explains its size: about five feet high, three feet deep, and a foot and a half wide. It was made of metal, had three or four drawers, and was extremely heavy when full.

It was also an inefficient way of storing information, and was replaced by the computer disk.

B

3 This machine is made of plastic and metal. It is small and light, because it was designed to be carried around. It is about one foot square and weighs five pounds.

The owner used the machine by hitting one of the metal keys at the front. This left a mark on a piece of paper that was rolled into the machine.

This machine was used for writing letters and reports. It was replaced by the word processor in the twenty-first century.

C

4 The fourth object is made of metal and powered by gasoline. It has a long handle, because it was used by people who walked behind it while pushing it around their yards. There were six metal blades at the bottom of the machine, which revolved while the machine was moving. It was used for cutting grass.

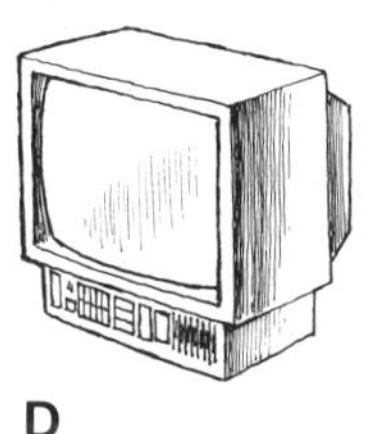

D

6 Writing

You are a historian working in 2090 and you have discovered these objects:

a washing machine

a vacuum cleaner

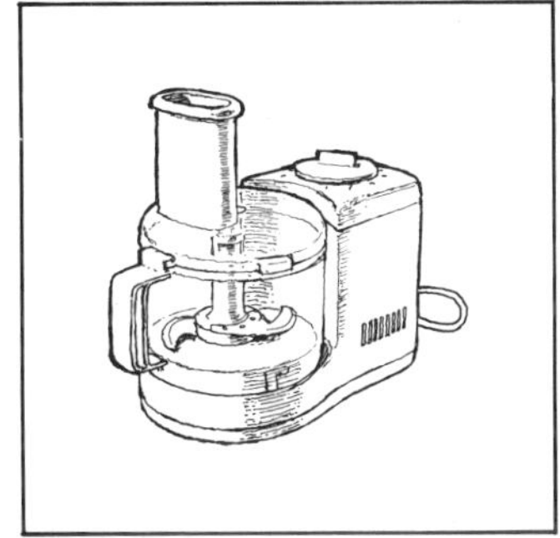

a food processor

a record player

Write a report similar to the passages in Exercise 5. Choose one of the items above and tell:
- what it is made of
- what it was used for
- what it looks like
- why it is not used anymore

New vocabulary and expressions

Vocabulary items marked * first occur in the *Interaction* or *Listening* sections of the Student's Book, or in the Workbook. Nouns are marked (n) to indicate usage in the text where confusion is possible.

Food/drink	*In the kitchen*	*Various*	previous	volcano
brandy*	to chill*	campaign	procedure*	to be willing to
garbanzo*	to mash*	to cast (cast)	to research*	wingtip
hummus*	to sprinkle*	child-care*	segment*	
juice*	to strain*	to choose (chosen)	simple*	
olive oil*		detail	snow(line)	
paste (n)*	*Measuring*	distance*	stuntman/woman	
puree*	length*	elementary school*	support (n)	
tahini*	narrow*	fuel	taxes*	
	ounce*	to get back to (you)	tranquility	
	thick*	to look after*	typhoon	
	wide*			

1 Review: spelling

There is a misspelled word in each of the following groups. Circle it and write it correctly. You may want to refer to the rules in the box; but remember: there are exceptions to every rule!

1 traveler (occuring) preceding arrangement *occurring*

2 polluted believe peacefull organizing ....

3 curlly investigator joking sadly ....

4 slippery casheir really attendance ....

5 definitely valuable changeable benefitted ....

6 spoonful piece vien practicing ....

7 nicest regretted admiting stirring ....

8 preference shiney flattest thief ....

9 annualy wrestling exaggerated gratefully ....

10 agreable preceding stealing caring ....

11 canceled choosing cheerful developped ....

12 reciept offended upsetting freight ....

- *i* precedes *e* except after *c* or when pronounced as *ay* as in *neighbor*: *relieve* (but *conceive*)

- drop the final silent *e* before a suffix beginning with a vowel: *ride—riding*

- when adding most suffixes, double the final consonant:
  a in a one-syllable word if the word ends in a single consonant preceded by a single vowel: *run—running* (but *sail—sailing*)
  b in a word of more than one syllable if the word ends in a single consonant preceded by a single vowel and if the stress remains on the last syllable: *refer—referred* (but *wonder—wondered*)

- when adding most suffixes, do not double the final consonant if the word ends in a long vowel, a consonant, and a silent *e*: *bite—biting*; *communicate—communicator*

- drop the final *l* when forming an adjective by adding *full* to a noun: *thank + full = thankful*

2 Review: *much* and *many*

Complete these conversations with *much* or *many*.

1 A: Serena hasn't shown ..*much*.... interest in the violin lately. Has she been

practicing ....?

B: She has so .... activities after school that she doesn't have

.... time for it.

A: How .... songs has she learned to play?

B: Not .... She's so busy that she hasn't had .... lessons.

2 A: How .... does it cost to send an airmail letter to the Philippines?

B: I haven't sent .... lately, but I know it depends on how

.... the letter weighs.

A: Here, feel it. How .... ounces do you think it weighs?

B: It doesn't weigh .... more than two ounces.

3 Asking about quantity

Complete Elliot's questions with *how far/fast/long/often/wide*.

ELLIOT: *How often*... do you visit your parents?

CARLA: We try to see them at least twice a year.

ELLIOT: .... did it take you to get here?

CARLA: Four days.

ELLIOT: .... is it from Salt Lake City to Phoenix?

CARLA: Oh, about 650 miles.

ELLIOT: .... did you drive?

CARLA: Our average speed was about 55 miles an hour, I guess.

ELLIOT: .... did you spend at the Grand Canyon?

CARLA: We were there for two days.

ELLIOT: .... is the Grand Canyon?

CARLA: The narrowest part is four miles and the widest is about eighteen miles.

ELLIOT: And .... is it?

CARLA: I'm not sure about the length. It must run about 200 miles. I know it's

huge!

4 Writing

Harold Gray's company wants to open a manufacturing plant in a small
southern town. Harold's boss has asked him to research two towns—Little
Falls and Los Perros—to decide which would be a better place for the factory.

	Little Falls	Los Perros
Population	21,500	4,880
Climate	Mild winters, warm summers	Very hot all year round
Unemployment rate	9 %	4 %
Local taxes	8.5 %	14 %
Schools		
Elementary schools	8	3
High schools	5	1
Average cost of one-family homes	$65,000	$80,000

Write Harold's report, comparing the two towns. Use these adjectives:
large/small, good/bad, high/low, more/few, expensive/inexpensive. Then
make Harold's decision: Where should the company build the factory? Begin as
follows:

REPORT

By: Harold Gray

Re: Little Falls vs. Los Perros

Little Falls has a larger population than Los Perros;

in fact, Los Perros's population is almost five times

smaller than

New vocabulary and expressions

Vocabulary items marked * first occur in the *Interaction* or *Listening* sections of the Student's Book, or in the Workbook. Nouns are marked (n) to indicate usage in the text where confusion is possible.

Emotional states
angry
depressed
shocked
thrilled

Regular verbs
to apologize*
to decorate*
to dismiss
to explode*
to insist (on)

to respond
to share*

The West
bullet
cattle
cowboy
to herd
ranch (hand)
revolver
rodeo

Various
to be on the rocks
to beat (beaten)
box office*
camper
to cash a check*
despite*
dirty*
financial
gossip column
hardcover*
hit (n)*

hospitality
jumbo jet
marimba
marriage
mystery*
object (n)*
otherwise*
paperback*
perhaps
promise (n)*
ridiculous
rock 'n' roll*

rumor
section
shortage*
spectacular*
to stand in line
   (stood)*
still (n)
streetlight*
subject*
wall
wedding
within*

---

1 Review: vocabulary

Write at least one noun that is derived from each of these verbs.

1 entertain *entertainer, entertainment*

2 persuade ....

3 complain ....

4 advise ....

5 suggest ....

6 compete ....

7 explode ....

8 organize ....

9 agree ....

10 describe ....

11 refuse ....

12 apologize ....

---

2 The present perfect continuous

Decide what each person is saying. Write the responses in the balloons.

1 Why are you so hot?

2 Why are you so dirty?

3 Why is the kitchen so messy?

4 Why am I so tired?

3 -*self* and -*selves*

Complete this conversation using reflexive pronouns: *myself, yourself, himself, herself, ourselves, yourselves, themselves.*

A: Is your husband here or did you come by ..*yourself*..?

B: I came by .... George stayed home with the kids. They're

too young to stay by ....

A: You and George ought to get .... a good baby-sitter. All

parents need to get out by .... every once in a while.

B: You're right, but we prefer to take care of the children ....

4 Review: *for* and *since*

Complete the story with *for* or *since*.

British composer Andrew Lloyd Webber has been writing successful musicals ....*for*........ twenty years. His biggest money-maker, *Cats*, has been playing in several of the world's largest cities .... 1981 and has been selling out in New York .... more than six years. The box office has been keeping special hours .... tickets went on sale for Lloyd Webber's latest hit, *Phantom of the Opera*. Theatergoers have been standing in line .... hours to see this spectacular production.

5 Writing

Read this letter of complaint.

```
Dear Sir or Madam:

I am writing to complain about your Customer Service department.

Last November I sent your company a check for $49.95 for a set
of records advertised on TV. I have been calling and writing to
you since then and after eight phone calls and six letters, the
records still have not arrived. Your Customer Service department
now says they have lost my order. This seems rather strange,
since you have already cashed my check.

The record store in my town sells only rock-and-roll records,
so I have been ordering classical records by  mail for the
last ten years. I have never had a problem -- until now, of
course.

I hope you will send the records within ten days. Otherwise,
return my money and I will order the records from someone else.

Sincerely yours,

Miriam Rostain

Miriam Rostain
```

Note the organization of Ms. Rostain's letter of complaint:

Paragraph 1: why she is writing (introduction)
Paragraph 2: what happened
Paragraph 3: why she is angry (explanation)
Paragraph 4: what she wants the company to do (action)

Now use these notes to write a letter of complaint:

To: A Book A Month

Complaint: 12 bestselling novels paid for 3 months ago, not arrived

Cost: $36.99 (check cashed)

*Written three letters, made five phone calls. No response to letters, nobody answered the telephone.

Explanation: Bookstores sell only paperback books.
                Have been buying hardcover books from A Book A Month since 1980.

Action: Want books in one week (sent Special Delivery).
          Otherwise, money back and will order from Reader's Guild.

New vocabulary and expressions

Vocabulary items marked * first occur in the *Interaction* or *Listening* sections
of the Student's Book, or in the Workbook. Nouns are marked (n) to indicate
usage in the text where confusion is possible.

Adjectives
cheerful*
consecutive*
convincing
current
enthusiastic*
gentle
graphic
impatient*
lonely*
majestic
recycled*
short-tempered*
tasteless*

People
architect
exchange student*
prince
principal*
sound engineer
vet

Places to stay
boarding house*
dormitory*
motel

Regular verbs
to aim (at)*
to bomb*

to express
to notice
to punish*
to separate*

Various
airfare*
amount
base
to be about to
to be in love with
clock tower
commentary*
definition
expense*

fire department
format
geography*
to get down
to get involved*
heat (n)*
item*
laundromat
levitated
link (n)
luggage*
magnet(ically)
market (n)*
material*
monument*

100-meter sprint
on the spot
portrayal
recipient
restriction
revenge
right away
right then and there
risk
row (n)
shade (n)
society
style*
to take a chance*
uncertainty

1 Vocabulary

Write a word or expression that logically completes each conversation. Refer to
the vocabulary box above if you need help.

1 A: The Prime Minister wants ...*revenge*............. for the attack.

   B: Of course. He insists on punishing the men who bombed the theater.

2 A: Did you make the decision .... , or did you think

      about it for a while?

   B: I decided right then and there.

3 A: Many school principals are asking parents to .... in

      their children's education.

   B: Well, don't you think it's time parents play a part?

4 A: Glass bottles and paper should be ...., don't you

      think?

   B: Yes, but many manufacturers prefer not to use materials again.

5 A: Don't stuntpeople .... serious injuries in their jobs?

   B: Yes, they take chances. But that's what they're paid for.

2 *Who, that, where,* or nothing?

Complete these sentences with *who, that,* or *where* when it is necessary. Do
not write anything unless you have to.

1 These are the pictures ...._–.–_...... I wanted to show you.

2 This is the girl ..*who*.... became an astronaut.

3 This is the house .... I was born.

4 This is the car .... my parents were driving when they had their terrible

accident.

5 That's the woman .... raised me.

6 This is the family .... I lived with when I was in college.

7 The town .... I went to college was very pretty.

8 Isn't this the little boy .... we used to play with?

9 I think he's the one .... broke the world record for the 100-meter sprint.

10 These are the pictures .... I look at when I feel lonely.

---

3 Categories

Match each description in column **A** with the appropriate category in column **B**.

A

1 artists: they shape figures from stone, wood, etc.

2 a sea: separates Europe and Africa

3 a Central American leader: he won the 1987 Nobel Peace Prize

4 an area in California: many movie stars live there

5 a place: the Pilgrims landed there in 1620

6 a bird: thought to be the smallest in the world

7 an Italian diver: winner of gold medals in 3 consecutive Olympics

B

a science

b entertainment

c history

d geography

e sports

f occupations

g international awards

---

4 Relative and contact clauses

These are the names and words that fit the descriptions in column **A** of Exercise 3.
Use the information to write sentences.

1 Sculptors *are artists who shape figures from stone, wood, etc.* ....

2 The Mediterranean ....

3 Costa Rica's President Oscar Arias Sánchez ....

....

4 Hollywood ....

5 Plymouth Rock ....

6 The hummingbird ....

7 Klaus Dibiasi ....

5 Writing

Josephine Da Cruz had a wonderful experience as an exchange student. Look at her notes and the article she wrote for her school's newspaper.

program — cheap: $800, 4 weeks including airfare and meals

teachers — excellent: helpful and patient, used interesting books, always willing to answer questions

housing — boarding house comfortable: my own room, shared bathroom with two other students (I hardly ever saw them!)

city — fascinating: many important monuments, ancient buildings and museums within walking distance of school

people — warm and friendly: one family invited me to dinner three times!

MY MONTH AS AN EXCHANGE STUDENT

The program that I chose was cheap -- only $800 for four weeks including airfare and meals.

The teachers that worked at the school were excellent. They were helpful and patient, used interesting books, and were always willing to answer any questions that the students had.

The boarding house where I stayed was comfortable. I had my own room and shared a bathroom with two other students that I hardly ever saw.

The city where I studied was fascinating. There were many important monuments, ancient buildings, and museums within walking distance of the school.

I think my favorite part of the trip was meeting new people. Everyone I met was so warm and friendly. One family invited me for dinner three times.

Sam Sadler was not as lucky as Josephine. Look at his notes and write about his experiences.

program — expensive: $1,300, 3 weeks including airfare

teachers — not very good: short-tempered and impatient, used old-fashioned books, never willing to answer questions; left room as soon as class ended

housing — dormitory uncomfortable: shared a room with five other students (they didn't leave the room except to go to class!), no hot water or heat in bathroom, food served in cafeteria cold and tasteless

city — boring: nothing to do or see, school located almost an hour from downtown

people — cold and unfriendly: no one interested in getting to know exchange students—nobody invited me to their home!

New vocabulary and expressions

Vocabulary items marked * first occur in the *Interaction* or *Listening* sections
of the Student's Book, or in the Workbook. Nouns are marked (n) to indicate
usage in the text where confusion is possible.

Adjectives	to deserve	atmosphere	handclapping	seatbelt buckle
adored*	to disappear	bridge*	itinerary	slave
lazy*	to donate*	childhood	lecture (n)	solution*
ordinary	to dream	cotton	limousine	tuba
typical	to mention	dock*	meditation	zoologist
	to provide	drug smuggling	misery	
Regular verbs		error*	period	
to bury	*Various*	executive	pollution*	
to collapse	according to	glory	preservation	
to decline	armchair*			

---

1 Using the dictionary: entries

Here are two dictionary entries for the word *ferry*. Identify the parts of the
entries using the words on the left.

spelling irregularities:
- simple past and past
  participle; present
  participle
- plural

part of speech = verb
part of speech = noun
pronunciation
stress
syllable division
takes an object*
example sentences
first meaning
second meaning

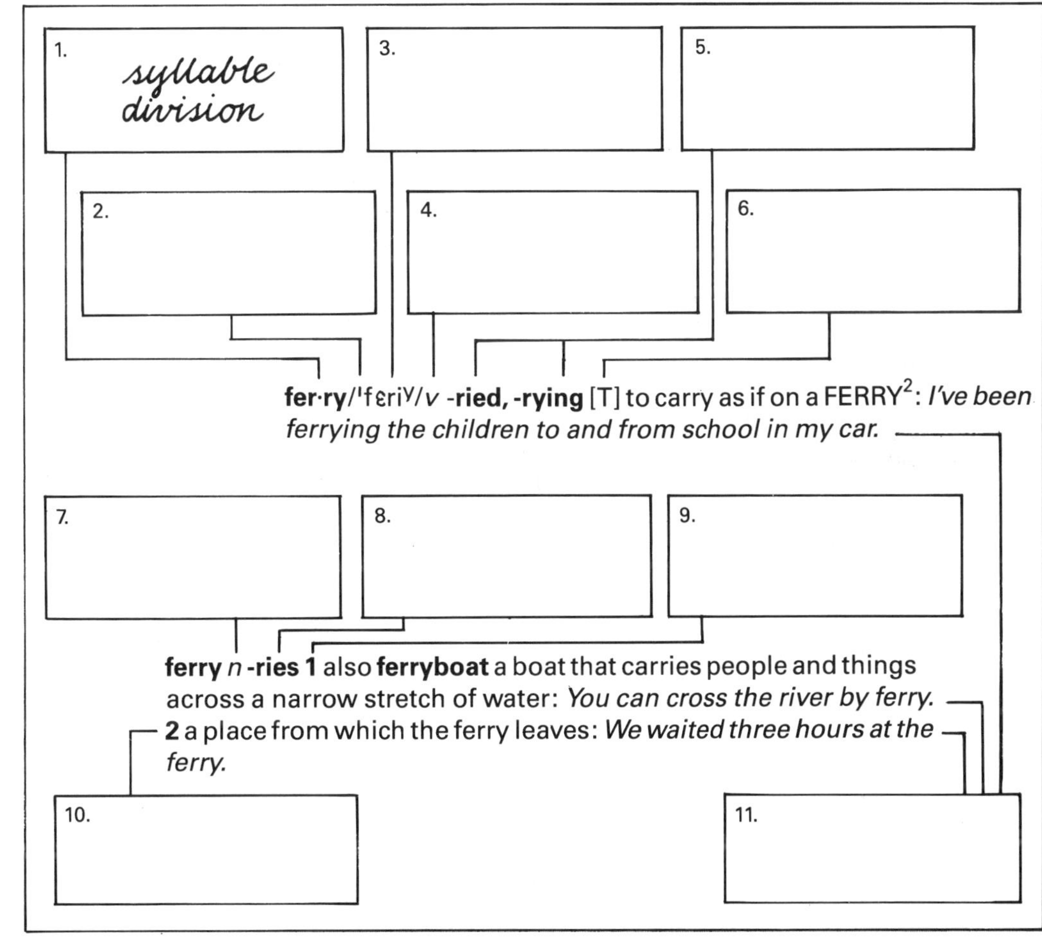

*Some verb entries are marked [T], indicating that the verb is transitive: it is followed by a noun or
phrase, or a direct object. Other verbs are identified as [I], or intransitive: these verbs do not have a
direct object.

Compare: fly *v* 1 [T] Mary flew her plane across the country.
          2 [I] Chickens can't fly, can they?

2 Review: tense check

Complete each of these short conversations with the most appropriate tense of the verb.

1 A: You speak English very well. *Have you been studying* .... for a long time? (study)

B: I .... studying English about four years ago. (start)

2 A: Lois .... for this company since she was twenty-one. (work)

B: I know. And her sister .... here, too, but she left two months ago. (work)

3 A: What were you doing when you .... the news? (hear)

B: We .... an old movie on TV. (watch)

4 A: My husband .... the *Daily News*, but he decided he preferred the articles in the *Times*. (read)

B: Really? I .... the *Daily News* for years now, and I think it's the best newspaper around. (read)

5 A: We .... to Japan before, but we hope to go next summer. (*neg.* go)

B: I wish I could go with you. I .... to travel to the Orient since I was very young. (want)

3 Review: the passive

Rewrite these sentences in the passive, keeping them in the same tense.

1 Someone will meet you at the airport.

You will be met at the airport. ....

2 They take the food to the docks in trucks.

....

3 They are discussing the problem right now.

....

4 We have mentioned the subject several times before.

....

5 Someone donated a lot of money.

....

6 They made a lot of errors.

....

7 Someone is repairing the washed-out bridge.

....

8 They will wash your clothes and return them to your room.

....

9 They have made a number of complaints.

....

10 Someone has already mailed your check.

....

4 Poetry writing

Write a short rhyming poem using at least one of these pairs of words:
borrow/tomorrow, friend/lend, jog/dog, crazy/lazy, danger/stranger,
long/strong, pollution/solution, adored/bored, breath/death, height/flight.

> I went to see a friend
> To see if she had money to lend.
> But she said, "If you want to borrow,
> You'd better come back tomorrow."

New vocabulary and expressions

Vocabulary items marked * first occur in the *Interaction* or *Listening* sections of the Student's Book, or in the Workbook. Nouns are marked (n) to indicate usage in the text where confusion is possible.

The economy
economist*
economy*
to export
import (n)

The environment
acid rain
chemical*
ecological
environmental
fertilizer*
garbage*
high technology

insect*
pesticide*
sulfur*

Various
to achieve*
agricultural
athlete*
behind
to book a vacation
candidate*
chairman/woman*
concerned (about)
contest

to cut down on
daydreaming*
expertise
to forget
gambler
government*
grain*
heart attack
homesick*
to hurry up
imaginary*
to increase
irritated
issue*

labor
law*
millionaire
nation*
neither
properly
to rely on
responsible*
robbery
to save*
sequoia
situation*
spider
summer camp*

suspicious
system
telegram*
tip (n)*
tree
university
vegetable*
vehicle*

1 Vocabulary

One of these vocabulary boxes belongs to passage **A** and the other to passage **B**. Decide which box belongs to which passage and put the correct words in the blanks.

1 ecological	editor	jungles
sulfur	forests	insects
chairman		

2 expertise	peace	import
high technology	relying on	agricultural
health		

A

Martin Kahn, [1] .... of Save the Earth Publishing Company, has hired a new

[2] .... to take care of books about

[3] .... problems in North America. Kahn is concerned about issues such as high levels of

[4] .... in our rainfall as well as the disappearance of [5] .... and other living things from our deserts, [6] .... ,

and [7] ....

B

One of our top economists thinks it is time to stop

[1] .... other countries for the

[2] .... products such as grain, fruits, and vegetables that we presently[3] .... Since our country is among the top producers of computers and other[4] .... , we must use this [5] .... to help our farmers. We must develop programs to improve our citizens'

[6] .... while working with other nations to achieve world [7] ....

2 *If* or *unless*?

Complete each of the short conversations with *if* or *unless*.

1 A: We'll be late ...*if*............. you don't hurry.

   B: We won't get there at all .... you help me.

2 A: Mr. Moses won't be able to meet with you .... you can get here by 4:00.

   B: Well, tell Mr. Moses that I'll be there by 4:00 .... I can.

3 A: You are all going to pass the exam .... you study.

   B: It takes more than studying. I'll never pass .... I stop worrying about it so much.

4 A: .... the service improves in this coffee shop, I'll have to go across the street.

   B: Maybe you'd get better service .... you left a tip.

3 Conditionals: Type 2

Complete these sentences by writing the verbs in the correct tense. Use contractions.

1 If you ..*earned*................ (earn) more money, we ..*wouldn't be*........ (not be) broke all the time.

2 If we .... (travel), our lives .... (be) more interesting.

3 If you .... (not buy) a new car every year, maybe we .... (save) some money.

4 I .... (borrow) some money from the bank if the economy .... (be) in better shape.

5 Actually, our financial situation .... (be) better if we .... (not use) our credit cards all the time.

6 I probably .... (feel) better if I .... (stop) daydreaming.

4 Word order

Write these sentences in the correct order: **a** with *if* at the beginning of the sentence, **b** with *if* in the middle of the sentence.

1 in the country / happier / I'd be / I lived / if

   a *If I lived in the country, I'd be happier.*

   b *I'd be happier if I lived in the country.*

2 a foreign language / I spoke / a better job / if / I'd get

   a ....

   b ....

3 here / differently / they lived / they'd think / if

a ....

b ....

4 so hard / she wouldn't work / she didn't love / if / her job

a ....

b ....

5 you'd get / you got up / on time / to work / if / earlier

a ....

b ....

6 if / we wouldn't be / the baby / so tired / didn't keep us up all night

a ....

b ....

5 Writing

Your Life magazine is having a writing contest. The question is: Who would you be if you could be anyone you wanted to be?

> **W**ho would you be — Christopher Columbus, Joan of Arc, Genghis Khan, Cleopatra, Beethoven? What century would you live in — the twenty-first or the fifteenth or maybe even the fifth? Where would you live? What would your occupation be and what would you do in your free time? What would you eat and what kind of vehicle would you drive?

Write your story for the *Your Life* magazine contest. The questions above are only possible ideas to use in your story. You can write about anyone you want.

12

New vocabulary and expressions

Vocabulary items marked * first occur in the *Interaction* or *Listening* sections of the Student's Book, or in the Workbook. Nouns are marked (n) to indicate usage in the text where confusion is possible.

In the courtroom	*Regular verbs*	to question	department store	spy
attorney	to advise	to rephrase	displacement activity	stationery
defending	to arrange*	to reply	earlobe	stay (n)*
guilty	to assure*	to tap	enemy*	stopover
judge	to claim	to tug	fabric	terminal
jury foreman	to clarify		friendship*	transcript
prosecutor	to continue	*Various*	major (adj)	van
to sentence	to dump*	ashtray	microphone	victim*
testimony	to exclude	bat (n)*	miniature	watchstrap
trial	to fasten	bill (n)*	official (n)	welcoming party*
verdict	to gasp	Celsius*	paper towel	yard
Your Honor	to install	close*	relationship*	
	to intervene	cooperation*	researcher*	
	to object	counter	reservation	
	to perform	demanding	scandal	

---

1 Writing direct speech

Write these sentences, using correct punctuation and capitalization. You may want to refer to the rules in the box.

1 where are the lightbulbs asked the customer

"Where are the lightbulbs?" asked the customer.

2 they're in aisle 3 said the manager

3 I can't find the window cleaner either said the customer

4 did you look in aisle 1 asked the manager

5 no but I will answered the customer

6 have a nice day said the manager

Direct speech records the exact words that people say. Here are some rules for writing direct speech:

- Put the words inside quotation marks: " "
- Begin the words with a capital letter: "Hi"
- Put punctuation inside the quotation marks: "Hi."

Note the position of the comma and full stops in these sentences:
—"Hi," she said. "How are you today?"
—"I'm fine, thanks," he answered. "Do I know you?"

2 Who said it?

Match the statements in column **A** with the people in column **B**.

A

1 "I sentence you to 20 years in prison."

2 "We have reached a verdict, Your Honor."

3 "Isn't it true that you and the victim were enemies?"

4 "I'm Carolyn Kramer, covering the Ricard trial for WQMX."

5 "The jury has found Mrs. Ricard guilty of murder."

B

a reporter

b prosecutor

c judge

d court clerk

e jury foreman

3 Reporting

Report what people said at a meeting last week.

1

Mr. Harris

2

Mrs. Standard

3

Ms. Leonard

4

Mr. Harris

5

Mrs. Standard

6

Ms. Leonard

1 Mr. Harris said *that the company was having problems raising money.*

2 ....

3 ....

4 ....

5 ....

6 ....

4 Reported speech: present and past main verbs

Complete the sentences in this box.

direct speech	reporting at the same time	reporting at some time afterwards
I'm living with my parents.	She says she *'s living with her parents.*	She said she *was living with her parents.*
I live with my parents.	She says she	She said she ....
I'm going to live with my parents.	She says she	She said she ....
I can live with my parents.	She says she	She said she ....
I'll live with my parents.	She says she	She said she ....

5 Direct speech from reported speech

Look at the newspaper article and write what Dr. Noya actually said.

Dr. Noya welcomed the visiting doctors to Cornell Hospital. She said that there was a close relationship between researchers in the United States and Europe, and she knew the friendship and cooperation would continue for a long time. She said that she hoped the researchers would enjoy their stay in New York. She assured the visitors that the city was a fascinating place with a lot to offer. She said that the hospital staff would be very willing to help the visitors and their families. She also said she looked forward to seeing everyone at the welcoming party Friday night.

Welcome to Cornell. There is a close

6 Writing

A group of foreign students are coming to your school while visiting your town on an educational visit. Write a speech welcoming them. Tell them why you are glad they have come (first visit of foreign students to your school; close relationship between your school and theirs, international friendship, etc.). Suggest a number of things they can do during their stay. Say you look forward to seeing them at the welcoming party (and when and where it is).

13

New vocabulary and expressions

Vocabulary items marked * first occur in the *Interaction* or *Listening* sections
of the Student's Book, or in the Workbook. Nouns are marked (n) to indicate
usage in the text where confusion is possible.

Doctors/Treatment
clinic
dermatologist*
disease*
mental illness*
obstetrician*
ophthalmologist*
optometrist*
pediatrician*
pregnant*
to prescribe*
psychiatrist*
rash*

sore throat*
specialist*
to specialize*
to treat*
vision*

Various
to abandon
Academy Award*
account
adrift*
awoke*
to be all right
blackboard*

companion
emotional*
employer
expelled*
fancy
form (n)*
gauge
generous*
to get along*
harbor*
helmet
hypocrisy*
informally*

jeans
junction
to make a date*
to manage (to)
narrator
nearly
neighborhood*
nightfall*
picnic*
plenty
to present*
quick-tempered*
regret (n)

related*
to shut
to swerve
tactfully*
upright
Walkman
What a shame!
wish
worse
zone

---

1 Vocabulary building: medical specialists

Read the definitions in the box. Then complete the sentences.

- A dermatologist treats diseases of the skin.

- A psychiatrist specializes in mental illnesses and emotional problems.

- An obstetrician cares for pregnant women and delivers babies.

- A pediatrician is a specialist in newborn babies and young children.

- An ophthalmologist is a doctor who treats problems or diseases of the eyes.

- An optometrist checks and corrects vision, or eyesight, by prescribing eyeglasses.

1 José has made an appointment with the *pediatrician*

because his six-year-old daughter has a sore throat.

2 Michio has a strange rash on his legs, so he's going to see a(n)

....

3 Ms. Gordon has been depressed for several weeks; maybe it's time she saw

a(n) ....

4 I think I have something in my eye, but I can't find it. I'd better see a(n)

....

5 We all know Dr. Lusetti; she's the .... who

delivered most of the neighborhood children.

6 Tommy can't see the blackboard unless he sits in the front row. I suggest you

take him to a(n) ....

2 Wishes: present and past

Write what each person wishes.

1 I don't have good eyesight.

I wish I had good eyesight.

2 Oh, dear. I was rude to my boss this morning.

....

3 I didn't study another language in school.

....

4 I'm always short of money.

....

5 I didn't do the laundry last night.

....

6 I made a date with a person that I dislike.

....

3 Conditionals: Type 3

Complete the sentences using the information below.

THE SUCCESS STORY OF MARCIA BRODSKY

1 *If Marcia hadn't gotten into trouble in school,* .... she wouldn't have been expelled when she was 16.

2 If she hadn't been expelled when she was 16, ...

....

3 ....

she wouldn't have met Suzanne Dean, who was directing the movie.

4 If she hadn't met Suzanne, ...

....

5 If she hadn't become a student at Suzanne's film school, ...

....

6 ....

she wouldn't have won an Academy Award at the age of 24.

4 Conditionals: talking about the past

Write what would have happened if things had been different.

1 I stayed up too late last night. I overslept.

If I hadn't stayed up too late last night, I wouldn't have overslept.

2 I didn't hear the alarm clock. I didn't wake up on time. ....

....

3 I had only an hour to get ready. I got really nervous. ....

....

4 I left the house in a big hurry. I forgot my driver's license. ....

....

5 I didn't notice the police car behind me. I drove 60 miles an hour. ....

....

6 I didn't have my license. I got arrested. ....

....

5 Writing

Read this description of Peter's youngest sister, Ginny.

Appearance
My youngest sister, Ginny, is five foot five inches tall, with brown hair and green eyes. She has glasses, but doesn't wear them very often. (I wish she would wear them more!) She dresses very informally and hates it when she has to wear a dress. In the winter she goes around in jogging suits and running shoes; in the summer she wears shorts and t-shirts.

Personality
It's hard to say what someone's character is like, but I think she's friendly, very generous, and likes being with other people, especially children. That's the good side. The bad side is that she's rather quick-tempered, impatient, and often offers her opinion when it's not necessarily wanted.

Likes and dislikes
She likes swimming, going out for dinner, going on picnics, watching TV, seeing movies, and reading bestselling novels. She doesn't like talking about politics, and she hates lying and hypocrisy.

Things I wish were different
There aren't many things I wish were different in my sister. We have always gotten along very well, except for a few typical sister–brother conflicts. In fact, I think we would be friends even if we weren't related. Sometimes, though, I wish she would keep her opinions to herself or that she would present them a little more tactfully. Oh, and I wish that she didn't live in the Caribbean—we don't see each other very often since she went to live there.

Now write a description of a member of your family, using the text above as a model.

New vocabulary and expressions

Vocabulary items marked * first occur in the *Interaction* or *Listening* sections of the Student's Book, or in the Workbook. Nouns are marked (n) to indicate usage in the text where confusion is possible.

Adjectives
dull
embarrassing*
expanding*
experimental
extinct*
formal*
literate*
logical*
mature*

resistible*
routine

Various
apart from*
behavior*
business
  communications
butterfly
to cancel*
to consider*

customer service
  department*
to earn a living
to get off the ground*
to last
to mail*
memo*
notice (n)*
novelist
operation

payment*
to replant*
slice (n)*
spare time
to stay up late
street artist
to take the day off
totally*
to turn off*

1 Vocabulary building: negative prefixes

When the prefix *in*, *im*, *il*, or *ir* is placed at the beginning of certain nouns, adjectives, and adverbs, the meaning of the word changes to the negative: *INactive* = not active; *IMpossible* = not possible.

The rule for negative prefixes is *il* before *l*; *im* before *b*, *m*, or *p*; *ir* before *r*; and *in* before other letters.

Put the correct prefix before these words.

1 *im*..polite

2 ....logical

3 ....credible

4 ....probable

5 ....mature

6 ....secure

7 ....responsible

8 ....practical

9 ....resistible

10 ....literate

Now complete these sentences with the negative words above.

1 .... people cannot read and write.

2 Edith's argument is totally ....; it makes no sense at all.

3 Harold and his friends are in college, but their behavior is so .... that most people think they are still in high school.

4 The stories published in that newspaper are too strange to be believed; they are really ....

5 Your daughter is very ....; you must teach her to be more sure of herself.

6 In many countries it is considered .... to ask a woman how old she is.

7 That's a very ....suggestion. How can we cross the river without a boat?

8 Companies that throw garbage into our lakes and rivers are extremely .... and should pay for the damage.

9 Although June was on a diet, the apple pie was ....; she ate two big slices.

10 It is highly .... that it will snow; it hasn't snowed here in April since 1935.

2 Reported questions

A lot of people asked Tim Kasey questions while he was waiting to see the doctor yesterday. Report what they said.

1 The receptionist said, "Do you have health insurance?"

The receptionist asked if I had health insurance.

2 An old man said, "Have you been waiting long?"

3 A pretty young woman said, "Do you come here often?"

4 The nurse said, "How long have you felt sick?"

5 The nurse also said, "Do you always wear three shirts at the same time?"

6 The doctor said, "Did the nurse take your temperature?"

7 He also said, "Why are you shaking?"

8 Poor Tim finally said, "Why don't you stop asking me so many questions?"

3 Reported speech

These changes often occur in reported speech when the speech is reported some time later.

direct speech (actual words)	reported speech
this/that	the
here	there
this morning	that morning
today	that day
yesterday	the day before
tomorrow	the following day
ago	before

For example: When does this bus get to Paterson? ⟶ She asked when the bus got to Paterson.

Have you seen Kim today? ⟶ He asked if I had seen Kim that day.

Write these questions and statements as reported speech.

1 "Are they arriving this morning?" Sue asked *if they were arriving that morning.*

2 "I saw Leo two days ago." May said

3 "Are you reading this book?" Joe asked

4 "Why are you leaving tomorrow?"   Pam asked ....
5 "I work here."   Ray said ....
6 "Did they call yesterday?"   Kay asked ....
7 "Did anyone see what I just saw?"   Tom asked ....
8 "Do you know this woman?"   Ana asked ....

4 Writing

Albert Santoni works in the Customer Service Department of the local gas and electricity company. Customers who have problems call to talk to him. After Albert listens to the customers' problems, he writes reports to his boss. Read the conversation Albert had with Ms. Lee and the report he then wrote about her problem.

ALBERT: Customer Service. Can I help you?
MS. LEE: I hope so. I received a notice from you this morning.
ALBERT: Oh? What kind of notice?
MS. LEE: It says my electricity will be turned off if I don't pay my bill within 24 hours.
ALBERT: Yes, well, how long has it been since you paid us?
MS. LEE: It's very embarrassing. You see, I have a small business and it has been difficult getting it off the ground. I sent the last payment two months ago.
ALBERT: And how soon will you have the money to pay your present bill?
MS. LEE: I can send you a check for the entire amount—but not until next week.
ALBERT: Let me check your record . . . well, your credit has been good until now. I can give you the week you need. But if we haven't received your check by next Friday, your power will be cut off.

CUSTOMER SERVICE MEMO

To: Sheila Le Blanc
From: Albert Santoni
Re: Carol Lee (Account #441111350091)

Ms. Carol Lee called at 10:15 this A.M. She said she had received a notice that said her electricity would be turned off if she didn't pay her bill within 24 hours. When I asked her how long it had been since she had paid us, she said that she had sent the last payment two months before. Then I asked how soon she would have the money to pay her present bill, and she responded that she could send a check for the entire amount -- but not until next week. I checked her record and found out that her credit had been good until now. I told Ms. Lee that I could give her the week she needed but that if we hadn't received her check by next Friday, her power would be cut off.

Now read this conversation and write a report to Albert's boss.

ALBERT: Customer Service. Can I help you?
MR. HILL: Yes, you can. I sent you a $2,000 deposit two months ago, and I want my money back.
ALBERT: Is this a home account or a business account?
MR. HILL: It's my newest restaurant—Hill's Hamburger Hut.
ALBERT: I'm sorry, sir, but we keep the deposits from new businesses for at least a year. If your account is in order ten months from now, we will return your deposit. With interest, of course.
MR. HILL: Oh, no, you won't. I need the money now. I want you to mail me a check by the end of the week.
ALBERT: I can't do that, sir. If you have a formal complaint, you should write to Ms. Sheila Le Blanc at our main office.
MR. HILL: Then that is exactly what I will do. Goodbye!

CUSTOMER SERVICE MEMO

To: Sheila Le Blanc
From: Albert Santoni
Re: Henry Hill (Hill's Hamburger Hut -- Account #1234646200012)

New vocabulary and expressions

Vocabulary items marked * first occur in the *Interaction* or *Listening* sections of the Student's Book, or in the Workbook. Nouns are marked (n) to indicate usage in the text where confusion is possible.

Around the house
appliance*
blinds (n)
contractor*
exterior
fence
frame
grass
interior
to leak
plumbing
repairs (n)*
roof

At the beauty salon
to curl*
to dye*
eyebrows*

fingernails*
to manicure*
to massage
to thin*

The car
brakes*
fender*
headlights*
muffler*
to realign*
used-car lot

Expressions
It's killing me!
to like the sound of*
to skip*
to take a raincheck
to tell one's fortune

Modern inventions
disposable diaper*
hovercraft*
non-stick frying pan*
personal stereo*
returnable spacecraft*

Various
annually*
blood pressure*
candle*
cause (n)
'cause (because)
to contribute
copy (n)*
to crack
dead-end street*
enclosed*

to examine*
to fade
genuine
to give up*
guardrail
hunger*
installation*
memorandum
to notify*
overalls
pile (n)
portrait
poverty*
press release
to re-cover*
reduction
to replace
roommate*

scratched*
seasick*
sharpener*
stained*
surplus
sweatshirt*
therefore*
vase
to warn*
to x-ray*

---

1 Vocabulary: idioms

Choose the sentence that summarizes or explains the situation.

1 I never thought Josh would finish the race, but he made it.
  a He won.
  b He ran well.
  c He finished.

2 We can't come for dinner tonight. Can we take a raincheck?
  a We'd like to come some other time.
  b We'd rather come when it isn't raining.
  c We can't pay for dinner tonight.

3 My feet were killing me, so I took off my shoes.
  a I was too sick to wear shoes.
  b I never wear shoes in bed.
  c My shoes were hurting me.

4 Mrs. Scott's doctor wants her to lose 20 pounds but has advised her not to skip breakfast.
  a Mrs. Scott shouldn't eat breakfast.
  b Mrs. Scott should eat breakfast.
  c Mrs. Scott ought to do exercises after breakfast

5 I don't much like the sound of your plan.
  a I don't agree with you.
  b I don't understand you.
  c I can't hear you.

6 We have fought very hard in the war against hunger and poverty; we must not give up now!
  a We must not wait anymore!
  b We must not stop!
  c We must fight for peace!

---

2 *Have/Get something done*

Poor Christine doesn't like the way she looks. Her roommate, Lois, gives her some good advice. Write Lois's suggestions using these verbs: *curl, cut, dye, manicure, polish, thin*.

1 My hair is too long. *Why don't you get it cut?*

2 My hair is too straight. ....

3 I hate the color of my hair. ....

4 My fingernails are cracked. ....

5 My nails are a strange color. ....

6 My eyebrows are too thick. ....

3 What needs to be done?

Sarah and Louis are having a dinner party tonight. Look at
the picture. What still needs to be done? Refer to the verbs
in the box if you need help.

cook   dust   light   put in water   set   vacuum

1 *The furniture needs to be dusted.*

2

3

4

5

6

4 Word order

The Roosevelt Clinic is preparing a brochure for their patients. Put the following words
and phrases in order to make the sentences in the brochure.

1 | to have | | taken | | it's important | | your blood pressure | | regularly |

It's important to have your blood pressure taken regularly.

2 | their chest | | often | | x-rayed | | smokers | | should get |

3 | must have | | children | | checked | | annually | | their ears and eyes |

4 | their teeth | | they | | twice a year | | should also have | | examined and cleaned |

5 | like | | a full examination | | done | | every six months | | to have | | many older people |

6 | also need | | their vision and hearing | | regularly | | they | | to get | | tested |

5 Writing

Jody Powell's car was stolen. A week later it was found parked on a dead-end street. Look at the report from the insurance company's garage and the letter that the agent wrote to Jody.

Georgie's GARAGE

Service Report
Car: 1988 Acura

PROBLEM	SOLUTION
Lights: Both headlights broken	Replace
Body: Left fender smashed	Rebuild
Paint scratched	Repaint
Engine: Muffler missing	Install new muffler
Brakes: unaligned	Realign
Interior: Seat belts removed	Put in new belts
Seat covers and rugs	Order new covers
totally destroyed	and rugs

TOTAL COST: $4,200.00

Dear Ms. Powell:

Enclosed please find a copy of the report prepared by our garage. As you can see, the damage to your car was extensive.

We will have the headlights replaced and the left fender rebuilt. In addition, the car will need to be repainted.

We will also pay to get the brakes realigned and to have a new muffler installed.

The seat belts were removed from your car, so we will have new belts put in. The seat covers and rugs were totally destroyed; therefore, we will have new covers and rugs ordered.

The repairs will take about two weeks to be completed. The garage will notify you soon.

Sincerely yours,

Bob Baker

Bob Baker

Interamerican Insurance Company

Maggie Roman also has an insurance policy with Interamerican. Her house was flooded last week during a serious storm. Look at the report from the insurance company's contractor and write the agent's letter to Maggie.

CONTRACTING BY **CARLOS**

Damage Report
Address: 1410 Northeastern Street

PROBLEM	SOLUTION
Floors: Wood damaged	Pick up old floor and put down new floor
Walls: Stained	Repaint
Windows: Several broken, frames ruined	Replace
Furniture: Sofa soaked	Re-cover
Rugs destroyed	Order new rugs
Kitchen appliances wet	Check and replace if necessary
Plumbing: Badly damaged	Repair

New vocabulary and expressions

Vocabulary items marked * first occur in the *Interaction* or *Listening* sections of the Student's Book, or in the Workbook. Nouns are marked (n) to indicate usage in the text where confusion is possible.

At a concert
crowd (n)
electrician*
rock band*
rock concert*
to set up*
stage worker*
usher*
to warm up*

Bad weather
foggy*
hailstone
tornado
twister

Regular verbs
to admit
to attempt
to celebrate*
to cram
to down
to fail
to measure
to mold*
to rap
to realize
to sneak*

Various
apparently*
ashamed
assistant
attempt (n)
backyard
barrel
to be careful*
bid (n)
bits (n)
bruise (n)
car maintenance
  course
ceiling
clay*

comic strip*
contestant
to count on*
couple
crossword puzzle*
cut (n)
debris
disappointed
to dive, dove
to draw (drawn)*
drawing (n)*
engagement*
fisherman
instrument
in training

nonsense*
obviously
offer (n)
plugs (n)
premier
puppy*
request (n)*
shopping mall
to skip rope
to strike, struck
Volkswagen (VW)
worst*

1 Vocabulary: two-word verbs

Many verbs are followed by prepositions or adverbs. These verbs form a verb phrase and are called two-word, or phrasal, verbs.

Fill in these sentences with the preposition or adverb that completes the two-word verb. Refer to the words in the box if you need help.

after   down   for   on   out

1 We've looked .. *for* ...... her everywhere.

2 We've run .... of flour.

3 If you need help, you know you can always count .... me.

4 The bank turned .... our request for a loan.

5 Why don't you ask the neighbors to look .... the kids while you go to the post office?

6 Grandfather insists .... eating tomatoes twice a day.

2 *Managed to* or *was/were able to*

Complete the sentences with *managed to* or *was/were able to*. Say if both are possible. Some sentences require a negative form.

1 When I was young, I .... skate pretty well, but I can't now.

2 Although it was very foggy, I .... drive to work.

3 After a long search, we .... find our dog, but we .... find her puppies.

4 Ali's brothers and sisters .... learn French, Japanese, and Arabic, but he speaks only English.

5 After trying for two hours, I finally .... complete the crossword puzzle.

3 Time clauses with *while* and *when*

Look at the pictures and write sentences describing what went on the night of the big rock concert.

1 *Some fans were waiting when the rock band arrived at the concert hall.*

(some fans wait) (the rock band arrives at the concert hall)

2 *The stage workers were checking the lights while the band was setting up the equipment.*

(the stage workers check the lights) (the band sets up the equipment)

3 ....

....

(the musicians warm up) (the singer gets dressed)

4 ....

....

(the ushers get ready to open the doors) (the lights go out)

5 ....

....

(the electricians fix the lights) (the ushers tell the crowd to wait)

6 ....

....

(the audience fills the hall) (two fans without tickets sneak in)

4 Writing

Jim Johnson, creator of several popular comic strips, wrote about how he became an artist.

MY PARENTS say they first realized I was going to be an artist when I was three years old. While all the other children were building with blocks and molding clay, I was drawing. My pictures always told a story, even before I knew how to write.

When I got older, I used to sit at home creating all kinds of strange characters on paper while my friends were outside playing baseball.

In my third year of high school, I had a wonderful English teacher named Mr. Ross. He liked my drawings a lot. It was Mr. Ross who encouraged me to write dialogs to go with my pictures. Thanks to him, the *Spooky* character was born. That was my first comic strip . . . .

Write a similar story about yourself telling how you became interested in something or someone. You may want to mention a person or an event that influenced or changed your life in some way.

New vocabulary and expressions

Vocabulary items marked * first occur in the *Interaction* or *Listening* sections of the Student's Book, or in the Workbook. Nouns are marked (n) to indicate usage in the text where confusion is possible.

Fairy tales
castle*
dragon*
fairy tale*
knight*
princess*
witch*
wizard*

Police work
burglar*
criminal record*
escape (n)
evidence*

to speculate
speculation*
suspect (n)
theft*

Regular verbs
to bark
to congratulate
to deepen
to overflow*
to reappear
to resign*
to succumb
to suppose

Various
antipollution laws*
apology
attitude
banned*
beached whale
to blow up*
burns (n)
buzzing
cashier*
cash register*
curve
detergent*

disappearance
edge*
employee
enforced*
express cleaners
floppy disks*
halfway
headline
journey
joyride (n)
to jump the tracks
lowered*
miserable

paperwork
recrimination
running shoes
shift (n)*
sunstroke
taxi*
topical*
towards
video player*
wallet

---

1 Vocabulary: synonyms

Look at the news stories in Exercise 3 on page 70 of *Coast to Coast* Student's Book 3. Find the words that mean the same or almost the same as these.

1 destroying ....

2 miles per hour ....

3 except for ....

4 newspaper reporters ....

5 blow up ....

6 pilot ....

7 fall with a loud noise ....

8 very frightened ....

---

2 Identifying parts of speech

Look at these headlines from Exercise 5 on page 70 of *Coast to Coast* Student's Book 3. How are the circled words used? Write their part of speech (adjective, verb, noun, adverb, etc.).

(Ghost) Ship (Mystery)

1 *adjective* .... **2** ....

(Lucky) (Escape) for Bus Passengers

3 .... **4** ....

(Beached) Whale Finally (Succumbs)

5 .... **6** ....

(Missing) (Painting) Found

7 .... **8** ....

3 Making suggestions

One way to make suggestions or recommendations is:

$$We \left\{ \begin{array}{l} recommend \\ suggest \end{array} \right\} that\ X + infinitive.$$

Look at these sentences:
The doctor recommends that Joe quit smoking.

The travel agency suggests that travelers take their passports with them.

Rewrite this paragraph changing the sentences to suggestions and recommendations.

City taxes should be lowered. The subway system should be expanded and improved. Trucks should be banned from the downtown area. All cars, except taxis, should also be banned except on weekends. Antipollution laws should be enforced. Finally, the mayor should resign.

We suggest that city taxes be lowered. ....

....

....

....

....

....

....

....

4 *Must have, could/couldn't have, might have, should/shouldn't have*

Complete the conversation with the correct form of the verbs in parentheses.

A: Why are you sitting in your car?

B: Joanne and Jerry aren't here. They *must have forgotten* .... we were coming. (must forget)

A: How .... they ....? (could forget)

   We've had this date for two weeks.

B: Don't ask me! All I know is that they aren't here. Where .... they ....?
   (could go)

A: Their car is here, so they .... (couldn't go) far. They

   .... for a walk. (might go)

B: I doubt that. Oh, look! Here they come. They .... jogging. (must be)

A: I told you they .... about us. (couldn't forget)

B: Well, they .... us to come at noon. (shouldn't tell)

   We .... to come later. (should arrange)

5 Writing

The Gumshoe Detective Agency is investigating a theft at a small import–export business on Bourbon Street in New Orleans. Look at Detective Gumshoe's notes.

Evidence shows (speculations):
* *the receptionist probably forgot to lock the gate*
* *the accountant possibly left the office door open*
* *almost sure that the cashier did not put the cash in the safe, and it is possible that she left the keys to the safe in the cash register*
* *the cash register was probably left open*
* *maybe the security guard did not remember to turn on the burglar alarm*
* *sure that the security guard did not work his entire shift*

Mistakes made:
the head of Accounting hired a cashier with a criminal record. Also she did not check the office before she went home.

Now write Gumshoe's report to his client. Begin as follows:

REPORT.

I still have not solved this case, but I have several speculations about how the theft took place. The receptionist must have forgotten to

---

SPECULATIONS
probably = must have
possibly
it is possible } = might have
maybe = could have
(almost) sure = couldn't have

RECOMMENDATIONS
should/shouldn't have

New vocabulary and expressions

Vocabulary items marked * first occur in the *Interaction* or *Listening* sections of the Student's Book, or in the Workbook. Nouns are marked (n) to indicate usage in the text where confusion is possible.

Contact with outer space
antenna
extraterrestrial
frequency
galaxy
to make contact with
observatory
planet
radio dish
radio telescope
rocket

screen
signal (n)
starship

Various
aboard
to analyze
antic
banquet
to be fed up*
boldly
capable of

capsule
communicative
convention
crown
depth
donation
exploits (n)
false alarm
famine relief
to flash
forbidden*
to gather

graduate student
to identify with
to jump into action
legend
lottery*
message
nonprofit
obsolete
original
political party
primitive
priority

profit (n)
questionnaire
series
simultaneously
to support
worship

---

1 Vocabulary: informal language

Rewrite this story substituting a more formal word for each of the underlined words and expressions. Make all necessary changes.

"My life has always been <u>tough</u>. <u>Yeah</u>, nothing seems to come easy for some <u>guys</u>. <u>How come</u> some <u>folks</u> are luckier than others? Even when I was a <u>kid</u>, I had to struggle. But yesterday that all changed, and everything's going to be <u>OK</u>. You see, yesterday I won the lottery, and I'm a millionaire!"

....
....
....
....
....
....
....
....

---

2 Defining

Write definitions in English for these words.

1 *Popular* means *well-liked*.

2 *Boldly* means ....

3 A *legend* is ....

4 *Drama* means ....

5 *False* means ....

6 A *relative* is ....

3 Review: test

Choose the correct answer and circle **a**, **b**, or **c**.

1 I'm very interested in .... the answer.
  a finding out   **b** find out   **c** that I find

2 A new airport .... at the moment.
  a is building   **b** was built   **c** is being built

3 The computers .... before they leave the factory.
  a are checking   **b** are checked   **c** checked

4 This place .... be a school before the war.
  a is used to   **b** used to   **c** uses

5 I'm fed up. .... for the bus since three o'clock.
  a I've been waiting   **b** I waited   **c** I was waiting

6 She arrived at nine and said .... sorry.
  a she is   **b** she had been   **c** she was

7 He left a year ago. He said he .... live in Paris.
  a was going to   **b** is going to   **c** will

8 We were looking at an empty room. Everybody ....
  a was leaving   **b** left   **c** had left

9 The conductor asked me if .... a ticket.
  a I'll have   **b** I was having   **c** I had

10 Nobody knew why ....
  a did she leave   **b** had she left   **c** she had left

11 This is the place .... we stayed on vacation.
  a that   **b** which   **c** where

12 He's the man .... you about.
  a I told   **b** who told   **c** that told

13 You'd be healthier if .... more exercise.
  a you do   **b** you did   **c** you'll do

14 If I were wrong, ... apologize.
  a I'd   **b** I did   **c** I had

15 You shouldn't do that in here. It's ....
  a allowed   **b** not allowed   **c** not forbidden

16 If I'd remembered, I .... called you.
  a would   **b** would have   **c** had

17 I wish he .... said that.
  a wouldn't   **b** hadn't   **c** didn't

18 I saw them .... at ten o'clock.
  a to leave   **b** they left   **c** leave

19 This room is very dirty. It needs ....
  a to clean   **b** clean   **c** to be cleaned

20 I have some money. I think I'll have my apartment ....
  a decorated   **b** decorating   **c** to be decorated

STUDENT'S BOOK 3 LISTENING PASSAGES

RADIO WQMX

UNIT 1

ANNOUNCER: . . . so that's the weather today—and remember, don't leave home without your umbrella. We'll be back with news and the traffic report after this.

WOMAN: Do you have those days when you just can't handle it? When everything seems to be getting you down? An important meeting, a necessary shopping trip, a social engagement you just can't get out of . . . and on top of all that, your head is simply throbbing with pain. That's right, headaches can sure ruin your day!
But not anymore! Because now there's Brain-lane, the new fast pain-reliever from Woodruff Pharmaceuticals. Brain-lane works in only seconds to send those nasty headaches away. No more pain, no more suffering, thanks to Brain-lane.

MAN: Brain-lane. The doctor's choice. Get yours today and wave those headaches goodbye. Brain-lane from Woodruff.

MAN 1: Where can I get a good dinner?
MAN 2: In this city? You've got to be kidding.
MAN 1: Yes, but I want something different. I love traditional cooking . . . but not every day.
MAN 2: Well, why not go to Pedro's Place?
MAN 1: Pedro's Place? What's that?
MAN 2: It's the greatest Mexican restaurant in town.
MAN 1: But I've had Mexican food before.
MAN 2: Not like the menu at Pedro's Place. They have chili, tamales, enchiladas, tacos, and wonderful guacamole.
MAN 1: Mm. That sounds good.
MAN 2: It is. It's the best Mexican restaurant around.
MAN 1: I'll go tonight. Hey, by the way, how come you know so much about Pedro's Place?
MAN 2: I'm the cook!
MAN 1: Pedro's Place. On Harrison and Canal Boulevard.

WOMAN: What did Michael Jackson say when his sister sang in a nightclub? How did Robert de Niro put on so much weight for his last role and how did he lose it again? What *did* Faye Dunaway say when she met Britain's Prince Charles at a White House reception? Find out the answers to these questions and many, many more when you buy *Stardust*, a weekly magazine that tells you all you want to know about today's stars.

MAN: And *Stardust* has more. You'll find articles on dieting, a travel feature on exciting trips to Japan, and a special survey on what women find attractive in men. So if you want to know what's happening in the glamorous world of show business and if you want to make your own life more interesting, buy *Stardust*, today.

WOMAN: *Stardust* is today's magazine. Buy your *Stardust* today.

UNIT 2

ANNOUNCER: Radio WQMX. The time is five after nine.

VOICE: Pearsons, the makers of Slimwheat cereal, now bring you "Living With Ourselves," introduced by Marion Kennedy.

MARION: Next time you go to a friend's dinner party, why don't you check on how the other guests are sitting? Yes, you heard me right. Look at the way they are all sitting down. Do they have their legs together? Are their legs crossed? Maybe one of them is tapping her foot up and down on the carpet. And how about you, right now? If you're sitting down while you're listening to this, are you rubbing your ankle with your foot, or do you have your legs crossed? I only ask because Professor Bob Greene from the University of Massachusetts says that you can tell how people feel by the way they sit. This is how his theory goes: if people tap their feet it shows that they have a lot of energy to burn—that they have to get rid of. Ankle-rubbers (people who are scratching their ankle with their other foot) are expressing anger. They're angry but they have no other way of showing it. If you want to see a very tidy person—someone very meticulous—look for a person who has twisted one of their legs around the leg of a chair. So, if Professor Greene is right, the way we sit shows how we feel and what we are. How about you? How do you feel, how are you sitting?
Oh, and just before I go, how about this for losing weight? Scientists at the University of Arizona say that fidgeting is a wonderful way of burning calories. That's right! People who fidget—foot-tapping, waving their arms about and that kind of thing—actually lose weight because of it. So Professor Bob Greene was right: foot-tappers really *do* have energy to burn! So if you're one of those people who just can't keep still, you're probably keeping yourself in shape. Isn't that marvellous? Maybe you won't have to go jogging ever again!
Anyway, that's all for today's program. See you soon, and remember, stay healthy!

UNIT 3

TRACY: You're listening to WQMX, your friendly station, coming to you from the heart of Delta country here in New Orleans. It's a lovely day and here in the studio it's even lovelier because sitting right next to me in the very same studio is Julia Demspey. Hi, Julia, it's really nice to have you on our show.

JULIA: Hi, Tracy. And thanks for having me on your show.

TRACY: Oh, it's a real pleasure. Of course, as all you listeners know, Julia stars as Charlene Moses in that best of all TV dramas "Destiny." Tell us a bit about the show, Julia, and about your part in it.

JULIA: Yes, well, I play the part of Charlene. She's . . . she's 19 years old right now and she's part of a big family. I have—I mean Charlene has—three brothers and two sisters.

TRACY: But she's the oldest, right?

JULIA: Oh yeah. And she's kind of the central, the focus of the action . . . it's all on her because when her mother left home—you know she went away with a jazz musician . . .

TRACY: Wait a minute. You mean, Charlene's mother left home and ran away with a jazz musician?

JULIA: Yeah, that's right. And so Charlene kind of took over the family, the running of the family. She took her mother's place, you see. And so she's struggling—I mean, really trying—to stay in school, take care of her kid brothers and sisters and her father, Sam.

TRACY: So Charlene is still in school . . .

JULIA: Yes.

TRACY: But it's difficult because she has to take care of her brothers, her sisters, and her father?

JULIA: Yes.

TRACY: Is Charlene at all like you? Do you like her?

JULIA: Yeah, I like her, I guess. I mean she's had some really bad breaks and she still goes on, complaining all the time. I wish she wouldn't complain so much! And, oh boy, I'd like her to do something about Sam (her father)—get him to play his part in the family and that . . . but yes, I like her.

TRACY: Is she like you, though?

JULIA: Well, we have the same accent, but that's just about it. I have a really bad temper, I'm afraid—not like Charlene at all—but I don't complain. I just get out there and do it!

TRACY: Julia, can you tell us: what's going to happen now? Is Charlene going to get kicked out of school, or is Sam going to start helping her more?

JULIA: Oh, Tracy, you know I can't tell you that! We're not allowed to say anything about the story.

TRACY: OK. So let's talk about you. But first, this message from Brain-lane.

WOMAN: Do you have those days when you just can't handle it? When everything . . .

UNIT 4

JIM: Now, we have a surprise for you here on WQMX. One of our listeners, Phyllis Simpson, has sent us a story and she wants to know if we'll read it on the air. And the answer is that we will. Right now, in fact. Here goes. The story is called "The Way of the World" and it goes like this:

Jacqueline was in the kitchen. It was fall and the October sun was shining weakly through the large glass window above the sink. Jacqueline was busy and the concentration showed on her face as she adjusted the controls on her food processor. She had only three hours left to prepare dinner. Jacqueline's grandmother stood in the corner, next to the large kitchen table. "I don't like that machine," she said. "When I was young, we had to peel everything by hand, yes, and do all our own cutting and chopping too. We didn't use to have all those machines like you do. And we did it better than the machines do, anyway."

Jacqueline sighed. It was the same thing every time her grandmother came to visit. She always talked about what she used to do when she was younger, and how terrible modern ways were. Last night, for example, Jacqueline had argued with her husband at dinner. Ray wanted to buy a new car, but Jacqueline had said that they couldn't afford it. After dinner her grandmother took her aside:

"When I was young, I didn't talk about money with your grandfather. He used to make all the decisions. Money was his business. I don't think you should get involved, dear."

Finally Jacqueline could stand it no longer and she turned to her grandmother in the kitchen and said,

"Grandma, I just can't stand it anymore. When you come and stay, you watch everything I do and you tell me how it was different when you were my age and you go on about how you used to do this and how you used to do that. Please stop."

Grandma was silent for a while. Then she said,

"My mother used to tell me what to do all the time and I'm sure yours still talks to you like that. It's the way of the world, so don't get upset, dear." But Grandma left two days later and went back to Kentucky.

Two months later the weather was really cold. Jacqueline's daughter Amelia decided to go skating and was about to rush out of the house. Jacqueline saw her and called after her, "Put your coat on, Amelia. You'll catch your death of cold." But Amelia didn't want to. Jacqueline called her back into the house. "Now listen," she said. "When I was your age, I never went out without a coat and my mother—your grandmother—used to get very angry at me if I did. And don't make faces at me, young lady. I never did that to my mother when I was a kid." Amelia put on her coat sulkily and ran out of the house. As Jacqueline sat for a moment staring into space, the telephone rang.

"Hello? . . . Oh, Grandma, how nice to hear from you."

Grandma had called to tell Jacqueline all the latest news from Sharpetown, Kentucky and about her neighbor and her dog and her house and what the man in the hardware store had said. Jacqueline held the receiver to her ear and smiled until her grandmother had finished and was about to say goodbye.

"Oh, Grandma," she said.

"Yes, dear, what is it?" answered the voice on the other end of the line.

"Well, Grandma, I just wanted to say I'm sorry."

"Sorry, dear? What for?"

"It doesn't matter. But you were right, completely right. And Ray and I want you to come and stay with us again as soon as possible!"

UNIT 5

JIM: Welcome to "What's Going On" here on Radio WQMX, all the news and information about entertainment here in and around the Delta region.

TRACY: Yes, and have we got news for you because on Saturday it's time once again for the great steamboat race. On Saturday at noon the cannon will fire and the *Delta Queen* and the *Mississippi Queen* will start off on their race which ends in St. Louis on the fourth of July. Be there for the fun and the celebrations at the riverside for this great occasion.

JIM: Now, are you in good shape? If you feel you can do it, why not enter for the charity Mini-Marathon on Sunday? Get your friends to sponsor you for every painful, hot, dusty mile and raise money for a good cause! Sounds great, doesn't it? It all happens in the Louisiana Nature and Science Park and there are still two whole days left to register.

TRACY: But the event of the week—and I mean *the* event— is the visit to our city by the Kodo drummers from Japan. They're on an eleven-state tour of the U.S., and believe me, they are fantastic.

JIM: Have you seen them before, Tracy?

TRACY: Yes, I caught them two years ago in Atlanta. And they are so beautiful. They have these muscle-bound bodies and their concentration is total. And the sounds they produce. Oh, wow!

JIM: But what do they play? Just drums?

TRACY: Yes, but every possible kind of drum you can imagine. The sound builds up and up and the rhythms are just—I can't find a word—

JIM: Well, it sounds as if you all have to go and see the Kodo drummers. They're here for only two nights at the Municipal Auditorium, so go and see them if you can. But hurry! Tickets are selling as fast as kids eat popcorn! Now, here we have news of a great chili cook-out. I've heard of chili cook-outs, Tracy, but what actually goes on?

TRACY: Well, contestants come from all over the South—and some from Mexico too. And they cook chili con carne—real hot and spicy. And the best cook gets a prize.

JIM: Is that all?

TRACY: Well, no, there are bands and dancing, but it's the chili that counts! You can find out more by calling the Chili Society on Canal Street.

JIM: Yes, and don't forget, folks, that the week after next there is an exhibit of Brazilian art and culture at the New Orleans Museum of Art. That should be absolutely wonderful, so remember to put it on your calendar.

TRACY: That's right. And don't forget to check your local newspaper for details on movies and other events.

JIM: Until next week, then, that's all for "What's Going On."

UNIT 6

TRACY: And now, Chuck, you're going to tell us about movies that you've seen recently.

CHUCK: Yes, thanks, Tracy. It's nice to be back on your show. This week I've been watching police thrillers at the Plaza Theater.

TRACY: Why police thrillers, Chuck?

CHUCK: Because the Plaza Theater is having a season of police and detective movies.

TRACY: Oh, I see. Which ones are you going to tell us about?

CHUCK: Well, I've seen three altogether. I started with that great classic *A Touch of Evil* made by Orson Welles in 1957. Orson Welles himself plays the corrupt police officer Quinlan who lives and works just on the American side of the U.S.–Mexico border. Charlton Heston plays the Mexican cop who gets involved in a murder inquiry and ends up defeating Quinlan and exposing his corrupt ways. Oh, it's a really great film with some excellent night scenes, especially the first incredible unbroken tracking shot down the whole length of Main Street. Don't miss this movie if you haven't seen it before.

TRACY: OK. That was *A Touch of Evil*. What else have you seen?

CHUCK: After Welles's classic I watched a film that I've admired for a long time, Sidney Lumet's *In the Heat of the Night*. This is about a black police officer from the North visiting a small town in the South in the 60s. The town is incredibly hostile to blacks and no one more so than the local police chief. The black police officer (named Tibbs) is played by Sidney Poitier, while the hostile police chief is Rod Steiger. At first the two men hate each other, with Steiger's police chief giving Tibbs a really hard time. But Tibbs uncovers a sordid tale of murder and in the process wins Steiger's respect. The whole film is surrounded by a feeling of heat and anger that remains just below the surface. Go to see it.

TRACY: Yes, it's one of my favorite movies too. What's your last one?

CHUCK: The last movie was altogether different, a French film called *Le Cop*. Philippe Noiret plays a middle-aged detective in Paris. He isn't an honest policeman; he takes money from all the criminals in his area. When he eats in a restaurant, he isn't given a bill . . . until a young policeman—played by Thierry Lhermitte—arrives from the country and has to work with Noiret. This country newcomer doesn't approve of the middle-aged detective's habits and the film is about whether either of them will change. It is extremely funny and ends happily—so it's wonderful entertainment.

TRACY: That sounds great, Chuck. I've seen *In the Heat of the Night* but I've never caught *A Touch of Evil* before. And I've never seen *Le Cop* either.

CHUCK: It's really good. You should really go and see it. In fact, they're all good. All three movies are about the battle between "good" and "bad" police officers: Orson Welles and Charlton Heston in *A Touch of Evil*, Poitier and Steiger in *In the Heat of the Night*, and Noiret and the younger policeman in *Le Cop*.

TRACY: Which one did you actually like the best, Chuck?

CHUCK: Oh, I think I liked *Le Cop* best this time around. But that's just because it was the only one I hadn't seen before!

UNIT 7

TRACY: Hi, Fiona, thanks for coming into the studio today to share your cooking ideas with us.

FIONA: Oh, Tracy, you lovely person! You know how much I love coming here.

TRACY: Yes, yes, I do. Now, Fiona, you've come in today to tell our listeners about two simple recipes, right?

FIONA: Yes. My first recipe is for a kind of hummus. It's called Hummus Bi Tahina and it's an Egyptian version of an Arab dish. Hummus is a kind of paste. You eat it by dipping bread or chips into it and believe me, it's delicious. It's eaten in many Arab countries and in Turkey and Greece. Now, the ingredients for this dish are as follows. You need half a pound of garbanzo beans, a cup of tahini and another of water, a little lemon juice, garlic, and two tablespoons of olive oil.

TRACY: So what do you do, Fiona?

FIONA: Well, you start with half a pound of garbanzos—you can get them at any supermarket—and you soak them in water for about 24 hours.

TRACY: That long?

FIONA: Yes. You must soak them for that long if you want them to be soft enough. After 24 hours, put them in a heavy pan—an enamel or iron pot is the best—and cover them completely with water, and cook them for three to four hours. Then when the garbanzos are really soft, you strain them and mash them until you get a fine paste.

TRACY: And now you can add the other ingredients, right?

FIONA: Yes. Make two or three garlic cloves into a purée, stir in the tahini, the olive oil, and the lemon juice. You can then add salt and pepper. All we have to do now is pour in water so that the mixture is about as thick as mayonnaise—not too solid, not too liquid. There, that's about right. Then we pour it onto a plate or into a shallow dish, and it's all ready. Why don't you try it, Tracy?

TRACY: Thanks, Fiona, I will. Mmm . . . delicious. That's something I'll definitely try myself. What was the other idea you had for us?

FIONA: Believe it or not, it's sugared oranges. I used to avoid oranges because I could never cut them up properly—they always looked terrible! But there *is* a way of doing it and it's like this. First cut your orange in half, and then cut each half into four pieces. Peel each segment and take off all the white pith—it doesn't matter if your pieces look a little messy. Now put your messy—but clean—pieces of orange into a bowl and sprinkle them with white sugar. And now the best way to eat them is to chill the pieces in the fridge and serve them up in wine glasses. And if you want, you can put in a little Cointreau—or maybe even brandy. And I've got a glassful here for you to try, Tracy.

TRACY: What a lovely idea. Very simple, but—just let me have a taste—delicious and just the thing after a heavy dinner, especially with this Cointreau!

FIONA: Yes, it is.

TRACY: Well thank you so much, Fiona, for coming to see us today. We'll see you next week.

FIONA: Yes, of course, Tracy. And thank you for inviting me.

UNIT 8

ANNOUNCER: Radio WQMX: and now it's time for the Jim Cobb show with your host and friend, Jim Cobb.

COBB: Hi, this is Jim Cobb on station WQMX ready to receive your calls on our weekly phone-in program. And we have our first caller, Mrs. Marcia Winters. Hi, Marcia.

MARCIA: Hi, Jim. Gosh, I am happy to be on your show.

COBB: Well, we're pleased to have you with us, Marcia. What can I do for you?

MARCIA: Well, I live on Railton Street and what I want to know (*she has a coughing fit*) . . . sorry about that, Jim.

COBB: Don't you worry, Marcia. Now just go on. What is it that you want to know?

MARCIA: Oh, yeah. Well, you remember that City Hall said—I mean, even the mayor said—they said we were going to get new street lights on Railton Street?

COBB: They did?

MARCIA: Yeah, they made a big deal of it. They told us we should be grateful.

COBB: OK, so what's the problem?

MARCIA: Well, the lights are still the same. They haven't changed a thing. They made all those fancy promises and nothing has happened. We still have the old lights, and it just isn't safe for folks to go out at night 'cause it's too dark.

COBB: That sounds bad, Marcia. What are you going to do about it?

MARCIA: Well, I don't know. I called City Hall, and they said the lights are going to be changed next week. But I just don't believe them.

COBB: Well, it could be true. They wouldn't have said that if it were a lie, now, would they?

MARCIA: Oh, Jim, you don't know the people at City Hall. They'd do anything, and hey, even last week they . . .

COBB: So that's Marcia's problem, the lights on Railton Street. And I wonder whether City Hall really is going to do what they say. Maybe somebody from City Hall will give us a call. Right now we've got a call from Fred Pully. Hi, Fred. What can I do for you?

FRED: Man, isn't it great? I mean the new record by Suzanne Vega. She's really amazing, just brilliant. Do you like her songs?

COBB: Well, they're not bad but it's not really my kind of music, I guess. But I'm glad you like her stuff.

FRED: I think you're missing out, I really do, Jim. I mean, her lyrics, I mean, it's just like poetry, and that voice. . . . But if you don't really go for her, that's OK. I just thought I'd call and tell you, that's all.

COBB: I'm glad you did, Fred. And now I've got a call from Mary Brown. Hi, Mary.

MARCIA: I fooled you, Jim. It's Marcia again.

COBB: Well, hello again, Marcia. How did you get back on the show?

MARCIA: I gave them a different name. But don't worry, I won't be long. I just wanted to say the lights on our street are a problem plus I didn't like the way you cut me off your show. I won't be listening to you again. Goodbye!

COBB: Marcia . . . ? You still there? Well, I'm sorry, folks, but she seems to have left us—but she'll be back next week . . . she always comes back. And now we have a call from a Mr. Forman. Hello, Mr. Forman.

FORMAN: Good morning, Mr. Cobb.

COBB: Good morning. What do you want to say?

FORMAN: Just this. Marcia Winters was right. We did promise to improve the lighting on Railton Street . . . I'm from the city engineers department . . . and there has been a bit of a delay, but we're going to start next Monday so if she'll just be a little patient . . .

COBB: That sure is good news for Marcia and all the other residents. Thank you, Mr. Forman.

FORMAN: Thank you, Mr. Cobb. Goodbye.

COBB: Goodbye, Mr. Forman. Nice of him to call and good news for those Railton residents! And now before our next call, let's listen to some music.

UNIT 9

MAN: Kids! Is brushing your teeth a drag? Do you hate your toothpaste because it tastes icky? Well, do we have something for you! New Multi-stripe from Philo Pharmaceuticals. What do you think of Multi-stripe, Kevin?

KEVIN: It's really great. It looks great and the taste—oh boy!

MAN: How about you, Karen?

KAREN: Oh, it's real yummy—it takes your breath away!

WOMAN: So don't delay. Remember that brushing your teeth is truly important—and with Multi-stripe, it actually feels good.

MAN: So, goodbye cavities, hello, Multi-stripe. Try some Multi-stripe today!

MAN 1: Calling all passengers to Islamabad, Istanbul, Karachi, London, Paris, Amsterdam, Bangkok, Manila . . .

WOMAN: Don't you just hate arriving at the airport to check in for your international flight? All those lines, delays, luggage restrictions. It happens every time.

MAN 2: But not anymore. Because at Air International, we've created a new concept for executives on the move. First there's our first-class priority check-in. Then there's our generous 60-pound baggage allowance. And then there's the flight itself. Peace and quiet in our two-by-two first-class section. And the excellent service of a gentle and courteous cabin crew.

MAN 3:	Try Air International, the airline that takes the pain out of flying.
MAN 1:	Hey, where are you going?
WOMAN 1:	I can't talk now. I'll see you.
MAN 1:	That's funny. Oh, hi, Jean. Where are you off to?
WOMAN 2:	Sorry, Harry. I don't have time to stand around talking. Call me later.
MAN 1:	How strange. Mary, Mary, where are you going? I've been waiting for you.
WOMAN 3:	Oh, you have? Well, I can't have lunch with you today, Harry. I have something better to do.
MAN 1:	But what? What's happening? Where's everyone going?
WOMAN 3:	Why, to the Tadway House summer sale, of course.
MAN 1:	Of course!
WOMAN 4:	So why don't you join Jean, Mary, and all the others at the Tadway House sale where you get quality clothing at the best prices in town!
MAN 2:	Tadway House. On the corner of Masson Avenue and the Promenade.
MAN 1:	If you want to dance to the crazy beat And your feet hip hop across the street
WOMAN 1:	If you want your house to be full of noise So you can dance all night with the girls and boys
MAN 1:	If you feel your life ain't getting better You can't sing a song, can't write a letter
WOMAN 1:	Well, there's only one thing that you can do So listen good while we tell it to you.
WOMAN 2:	One two three four
MAN 1, WOMAN 1:	Just direct your feet to Basie's store There's records and tapes and much much more We've got CD's, Walkmen, stereo gear, And all the music you'd like to hear. So come on. Come on. Come on down To Basie's store on the east side of town. Come on. Come on. Come on down To Basie's store on the east side of town.
MAN 2:	Basie's music stores for records, tapes, CD's and audio equipment.

ACAPULCO VACATION

UNIT 10

ANNOUNCER:	Acapulco Vacation. A radio drama in nine parts starring Susan Holbrook as Jessica Marley and Courtney Frost as Amy Rosario. Part 1: A Good-Looking Man.

In a newspaper office

ELLIOT:	(*speaking on the telephone*) Hey, listen, Mr. Frinklestein. . . . I'm sorry you're upset but we have a job to do. . . . What? . . . Yes, of course we're going to run the story. . . . What? . . . No, Mr. Frinklestein, you listen to me. The *Daily Reporter* is a darned good newspaper and this is a story we are going to print. Goodbye! (*slams down phone*) Well, Amy—and Jessica—what do you two want?
AMY:	It's about our vacation, Mr. Elliot.
ELLIOT:	Vacation? What are you talking about? (*shouting*) Marlene! Can you bring me some coffee, please? Now, what's this all about?

AMY:	Well, if you remember, we're taking our vacation next week.
ELLIOT:	But you've only been here for six months—and you're training to be journalists. Why do you need a vacation?
AMY:	Mr. Elliot, we joined the newspaper immediately after we graduated from college and you told us then that we could have a week's vacation after six months.
ELLIOT:	I did?
JESSICA:	Yes, you did.
ELLIOT:	OK, OK. Maybe I did. Where are you going, anyway?
JESSICA:	Down to Mexico.
ELLIOT:	Mexico?
AMY:	Yes, Mr. Elliot. This time on Monday we'll be sunbathing in Acapulco.
ELLIOT:	OK, OK. You kids are just lucky, I guess. I hope you have a great vacation, Amy—and you too, Jessica. Now move out of here. I have work to do. (*shouting*) Marlene! Where's that coffee?
AMY:	Come on, Jessica. Let's go before he changes his mind.
JESSICA:	Next stop, Acapulco!

In Acapulco

JESSICA:	Oh, this is incredible. I could lie here forever!
AMY:	Jessica! You see that guy lying just behind us?
JESSICA:	What? You mean the good-looking one?
AMY:	Yes, that's the one.
JESSICA:	Well, what about him?
AMY:	He's been watching us for the last ten minutes and I think he's been listening to our conversation.
JESSICA:	Oh. Well, maybe he thinks we look interesting or something.
AMY:	Or something!
JESSICA:	Anyway, Amy, what should we do tomorrow? I'd like to try waterskiing. I swear I'll—
AMY:	We'll discuss that later, Jessica. Right now we can start getting ready for the man who's been watching us. He's gotten up and he's coming over here.

UNIT 11

ANNOUNCER:	Acapulco Vacation. A radio drama in nine parts starring Susan Holbrook as Jessica Marley and Courtney Frost as Amy Rosario. Jessica and Amy, two trainee journalists at a New Orleans newspaper, have gone to Mexico for their vacation. In Acapulco a good-looking man watches them on the beach. He comes toward them. Part 2: Mitch's Story.

In Acapulco

MITCH:	Excuse me!
JESSICA:	Yes?
MITCH:	Can I join you?
AMY:	I can't see why you . . .
JESSICA:	Yes, of course. Sit down, please.
MITCH:	Thanks. Listen . . . uh . . . I was lying over there—
AMY:	Yes, we know. We saw you.
MITCH:	Yes. And you see, I overheard your conversation. I mean, I was listening to what you said.
JESSICA:	Yes, we know that too.
MITCH:	OK, I'm sorry, but you see I heard you talking about your work, and . . . you're journalists, right?

AMY:	Well, yes, in a way. We're trainee reporters for a newspaper called the *Daily Reporter* in New Orleans.
MITCH:	Yes, I know that paper. The thing is, I have a story that I want to tell somebody about. A story that will be big news when people read it on their front pages. If I tell you, can you make sure that it gets into your newspaper?
AMY:	We can try. We can speak to the editor, at least. But wait, who are you? What's this all about?
MITCH:	Oh, yes . . . I'm sorry. My name's Mitch. Mitch Carlton. I'm a—I mean, I *was* a research chemist in Dallas, with a company called Eastward Chemicals.
AMY:	What kind of work did you do?
MITCH:	All kinds, but mostly tests on fertilizers and pesticides, that kind of thing. But I'm going to stop them.
JESSICA:	What do you mean?
MITCH:	I mean, I have a story about Eastward, and I'll tell you all about it. I've been silent for too long. But if Eastward finds out that I've spoken to you, that I told you all about it—well, I'm scared of what might happen to me.
AMY:	Oh, come on! You're being a bit overdramatic, aren't you?
MITCH:	Maybe I am. But you don't know Harvey Freeman.
JESSICA:	Who's he?
MITCH:	The president of Eastward—and he'll stop at nothing, I mean nothing. He's a terrible man.

Later, in a restaurant

JESSICA:	I still don't understand why Mitch is in danger.
AMY:	Well, after Eastward has made their fertilizers and pesticides, they have to get rid of the chemical waste products that are left over.
JESSICA:	Sort of like chemical garbage?
AMY:	Yes, that's it. The chemical garbage—as you call it—has to be destroyed. But they don't want to burn it because that would be too expensive. So someone from Eastward Chemicals takes barrels of the stuff out to sea and throws them in.
JESSICA:	And that's dangerous?
AMY:	Yes, extremely dangerous. After a few years of that, we'll all be eating poisoned fish—that is if there are any fish left. And anyway it's against the law.
JESSICA:	So if the press or the public discovered that they were throwing chemicals into the sea, Eastward would have to pay huge fines. The government might even shut them down.
AMY:	And that's why Mitch thinks he's in danger now that he's told us about it.
JESSICA:	Poor Mitch. So that's why he came to Acapulco: to think it over and hide.
AMY:	You like him, don't you.
JESSICA:	Yes. Yes, I think I do.

UNIT 12

ANNOUNCER:	Acapulco Vacation. A radio drama in nine parts starring Susan Holbrook as Jessica Marley and Courtney Frost as Amy Rosario. The two trainee reporters, Jessica and Amy, have met Mitch Carlton in Acapulco. He has told them that he is in danger because he has

information about a chemical company, Eastward Chemicals.
Part 3: Mr. Freeman.

Dallas, Texas

JESSICA:	Amy, this isn't a good idea.
AMY:	Don't be silly! We're following a good story! We're going to interview the president of Eastward Chemicals about the pollution of the sea.
JESSICA:	Yes, I know what we're going to do, but what about Mitch?
AMY:	Don't worry, Jessica. We're not going to put Mitch in any danger. We won't have to mention him at all. Mr. Freeman thinks we're just two trainee reporters learning our job.
JESSICA:	I can't believe he agreed to see us!
AMY:	Oh, Jessica! Didn't you know? The owner of the *Daily Reporter* is Freeman's brother-in-law. That's why Bill Elliot fixed up this interview for us.
JESSICA:	Well, then I guess it's a good thing that he doesn't know about Mitch.
AMY:	Here we are, Jessica. The Eastward Building. Come on. Let's see what we can find out.

In Mr. Freeman's office

FREEMAN:	And you've just come back from a vacation in . . . uh . . . Acapulco, I believe.
JESSICA:	Yes. How did you know that, Mr. Freeman, sir?
FREEMAN:	Oh, I think your editor mentioned it to my secretary when he called to make an appointment for you to come in.
JESSICA:	Oh!
AMY:	Anyway, it's very kind of you to see us, Mr. Freeman.
FREEMAN:	You're welcome. I'm happy to help people like yourselves who are training to be reporters. But I don't really have much time, so maybe you could tell me what you want to talk about.
JESSICA:	Chemical waste. That's what we're interested in.
AMY:	Yes, Mr. Freeman. Could you tell us how *you* destroy chemical waste?
FREEMAN:	Ah. Yes. Well, the chemical waste products have to be burned at a very high temperature and with special equipment.
JESSICA:	And is that done here?
FREEMAN:	Oh, no. First of all, the waste material is put into special safety containers and taken to our warehouse near Houston. There it's loaded onto trucks and taken to Brownsville, where it's burned at exactly 1,150 degrees Celsius.
AMY:	That must be very expensive!
FREEMAN:	Yes, it is.
AMY:	Is it cheaper to dump the containers into the sea?
FREEMAN:	It would be, but we can't do that—it's against the law, as I'm sure you know.
AMY:	Are you sure you can't, Mr. Freeman? Isn't it true that you dump the chemicals into the sea in the Gulf of Mexico?
FREEMAN:	Now, Miss Rosario, that just isn't true. We send our dangerous chemicals to Houston, as I told you.
AMY:	That's not what we've heard, Mr. Freeman. We've heard that somebody takes the containers out on a ship and throws them over the side at night—so that nobody can see.
FREEMAN:	I don't know where you got that story—or maybe I do. But I don't think you should try and write anything about "stories" like that. . . . I think I

might have to talk to your editor if you do—Mr. Elliot is his name, I believe. Yes. I think you should consider your responsibilities—and your future—as journalists very carefully in a case like this.

UNIT 13

ANNOUNCER: Acapulco Vacation. A radio drama in nine parts starring Susan Holbrook as Jessica Marley and Courtney Frost as Amy Rosario. The two trainee reporters have spoken to Harvey Freeman, the president of Eastward Chemicals, about chemical dumping at sea. He has told them not to continue with their story.
Part 4: Facts and Photographs.

Mr. Freeman's office
FREEMAN: Ms. Smithers!
SECRETARY: Yes, Mr. Freeman?
FREEMAN: Call Saul Brando. Tell him to come to my office as quickly as possible!

Outside the Eastward Building
JESSICA: Well, what did you think of Mr. Freeman?
AMY: He's a scary man. And I think he knows who told us about Eastward.
JESSICA: Yes.
AMY: I'm a little scared! Maybe we're in danger! It's a good thing he doesn't know where Mitch is.
JESSICA: But he does! Bill Elliot told his secretary! Mr. Freeman knows that we've just gotten back from Acapulco, so he probably guesses that Mitch is in Acapulco and that's where we got the story! We've got to warn Mitch!
AMY: Yes, you're right. But first we're going to talk to our editor.

In the newspaper office
ELLIOT: What do you think you're talking about? I'm not going to print your "story" in this newspaper. I want to keep my job, you know.
AMY: But Mr. Elliot . . .
ELLIOT: Could you bring me another cup of coffee, Marlene? Sorry, Miss Rosario, you were saying?
AMY: This is the *Daily Reporter*, the newspaper that always prints the truth. So why not print our story? Or is it because the owner of the newspaper is Harvey Freeman's brother-in-law?
ELLIOT: Well, that doesn't help, of course. But look, I arranged the interview for you to help you with your training. And you go and argue with Harvey Freeman. You've really gotten me into trouble. I mean, how would you feel . . .
JESSICA: I thought this was an independent newspaper.
ELLIOT: Now listen, you two. You come in here with a story about Eastward, one of the biggest chemical companies in the country. And you don't have any proof. No proof at all—no facts. No photographs. What do you expect me to do?
JESSICA: But Mitch! What about Mitch Carlton?
ELLIOT: He's the . . . what is it . . . research chemist, right?
JESSICA: Yes, and he's in great danger, because—
ELLIOT: Look, Miss Rosario. I was young once, just like you—I know it's difficult to believe—and I used to think that every story I heard was the most important story in the world. But I was often wrong!

AMY: But we're not wrong—and our age has nothing to do with it.
ELLIOT: All right, I tell you what I'll do. You bring me a story—with facts and photographs. If your friend Mitch Carlton has told you the truth, you'll both get permanent jobs with the *Daily Reporter*. If not . . . you can find another newspaper to work for.

At Eastward Chemicals
SECRETARY: Saul Brando is here, Mr. Freeman.
FREEMAN: Thank you, Ms. Smithers. You can go home now.
SECRETARY: Thank you, Mr. Freeman.
FREEMAN: Brando! Come in here quickly—and shut the door.
BRANDO: Right.
FREEMAN: Now, listen. I've got a problem. Somebody has told two young reporters about our chemical dumping in the gulf. And I think that somebody is Mitch Carlton.
BRANDO: What are you going to do?
FREEMAN: I'll tell you that in a minute. But at least I think I know where Mitch Carlton is.

UNIT 14

ANNOUNCER: Acapulco Vacation. A radio drama in nine parts starring Susan Holbrook as Jessica Marley and Courtney Frost as Amy Rosario. Jessica and Amy, the two reporters, have interviewed Harvey Freeman about the dumping of dangerous chemicals into the sea. They want their editor to print the story in his newspaper, and they are worried about their friend Mitch Carlton.
Part 5: Be Careful.

The phone rings
JESSICA: Come on! Come on, Mitch, answer the phone.
MITCH: Hello.
JESSICA: Hello. Mitch? Is that you?
MITCH: Who is this?
JESSICA: Mitch, it's me, Jessica Marley.
MITCH: Oh, Jessica. I hoped you would call.
JESSICA: Are you OK, Mitch?
MITCH: Yes, of course. What's wrong?
JESSICA: Oh, Mitch. I've been trying to call you for the last three hours, but you haven't answered.
MITCH: I haven't been here. I've been shopping—I bought a new typewriter—and I'm going to write down everything I know about Eastward and their sea dumping—and I've . . . well . . .
JESSICA: What? What, Mitch?
MITCH: I've been thinking about you a lot.
JESSICA: I've been thinking about you too, Mitch. But I'm calling to warn you.
MITCH: Warn me? What about?
JESSICA: You have to leave Acapulco.
MITCH: Why?
JESSICA: Oh, Mitch, I'm sorry. But we weren't thinking. We went to Eastward and we talked to Mr. Freeman—
MITCH: You did *what*?
JESSICA: —and we asked him about dumping chemicals at sea. And he denied everything. But someone told him that we'd just been to Acapulco, so he must realize that you are there and . . .
MITCH: So they know where I am, do they?
JESSICA: Yes, Mitch. So please, please leave Acapulco.

MITCH: How could you go and talk to Freeman? How could you be so stupid?

JESSICA: Mitch, I'm sorry, but it's done now and we can't change it. You're in danger, so get out of Acapulco. Soon. Please.

MITCH: All right, I will. But what are you going to do?

JESSICA: Amy and I are going to Houston to see if your story is true.

MITCH: Of course it's true. Don't tell me you don't believe me anymore!

JESSICA: Of course I believe you. Now, about that warehouse with the green roof, and the boat called the *Tampa Queen* . . .

MITCH: Never mind. I don't think you should get involved. Don't go asking any more questions. It's not worth it.

JESSICA: We're not going to do very much. We're just going to drive down to Houston and have a look around —maybe we'll even see the *Tampa Queen*.

MITCH: Jessica, for heaven's sake. Stay out of it. Stay away from Eastward and Freeman. They're dangerous!

JESSICA: I know, but we'll be OK. I have to go now, Mitch. Call me the day after tomorrow.

MITCH: Jessica? Jessica? Please be careful . . .

At Eastward Chemicals

FREEMAN: So that's the situation, Brando. These two girls— they say they're reporters—know about the dumping operation in the Gulf of Mexico. And Mitch Carlton told them about it. I'm sure of that.

BRANDO: So what do you want me to do, Mr. Freeman?

FREEMAN: Get one of your men to follow those girls. I want to know where they go, what they do, and who they see.

BRANDO: And Mitch Carlton?

FREEMAN: I want you to take a little trip to Acapulco. Find Carlton and then make sure that he has an accident.

BRANDO: You mean . . . ?

FREEMAN: Yes, Brando, I mean, silence him. Forever.

UNIT 15

ANNOUNCER: Acapulco Vacation. A radio drama in nine parts starring Susan Holbrook as Jessica Marley and Courtney Frost as Amy Rosario. Jessica has called Mitch Carlton in Acapulco to warn him about Harvey Freeman. Freeman knows where Mitch is, and he knows that Mitch told Jessica and Amy about the chemical dumping at sea. Jessica and Amy are on their way to see the Eastward warehouse near Houston.
Part 6: Joseph.

In the car

JESSICA: This rain is incredible. I've never seen weather like this at this time of year.

AMY: The road forks here, Jessica. Do I turn right or left?

JESSICA: Uh . . . left, I guess.

AMY: Are you sure?

JESSICA: Oh no! I mean right, of course. I was reading the map upside down!

AMY: Oh, Jessica! We'll turn right, then. What does the Eastward warehouse look like?

JESSICA: Mitch said it had a green roof. And he said that the containers were taken straight from the warehouse to a ship called the *Tampa Queen*.

AMY: We'll soon find out if he's right.

JESSICA: Look. That's the warehouse with the green roof and they're loading those barrels onto the *Tampa Queen*.

AMY: Yes. They must be full of chemical waste. Look at the symbols on the side of the barrels. It looks as if Mitch was right.

JESSICA: Of course he was right. But what are we going to do about it?

AMY: We're going to see that friend of his. Joseph, I think his name was.

JESSICA: Yes, but . . .

AMY: Mitch said Joseph would help us. And he has his own fishing boat. We have to persuade him to take us out to sea.

JESSICA: But what can he do? Look at the weather!

AMY: Don't worry about the weather. We're going to follow the *Tampa Queen* when she leaves port.

JESSICA: But I get seasick!

In a workshop

FRED: Hey, Joseph. There are a couple of ladies outside who want to see you.

JOSEPH: Ladies?

FRED: Yeah. They say they're friends of Mitch Carlton's.

JOSEPH: Oh, well. Any friend of Mitch's is a friend of mine. Show them in.

JOSEPH: I'm sorry. I'm not taking you out there in my boat. Not today. Not in this weather. And that's final.

AMY: But, Joseph, Mitch said that you would help. And he's in terrible trouble.

JESSICA: Yes. Mitch said that you were his best friend—the only person who would help without thinking about it twice.

JOSEPH: Well . . . yes, but . . .

AMY: Come on, Joseph. We don't have to go out far.

JESSICA: Yes. Come on, Joseph. For Mitch's sake.

JOSEPH: OK, OK. Now get into those clothes—and put on lifejackets. You'll probably need them. I must be crazy!

From a payphone at the port

MAN: Hello. Mr. Freeman. Those girls have just left.

FREEMAN: Left? What do you mean?

MAN: They're on a fishing boat—and they're following the *Tampa Queen* out of the port.

FREEMAN: Oh, they are, are they? I'll radio the *Tampa Queen*'s captain. This has got to stop!

UNIT 16

ANNOUNCER: Acapulco Vacation. A radio drama in nine parts starring Susan Holbrook as Jessica Marley and Courtney Frost as Amy Rosario. Jessica and Amy watched barrels of chemical waste being loaded onto the ship the *Tampa Queen*. They have followed the ship out to sea in a boat owned by Mitch Carlton's friend Joseph, but they have been seen.
Part 7: The *Tampa Queen*.

On Joseph's boat

JESSICA: Ohh . . . aah . . . this is terrible.

AMY: Are you OK, Jessica?

JESSICA: No. I'm dying.

JOSEPH: You may think so, but you're just seasick.
JESSICA: Oh, is that all? . . . Oh, excuse me, I think I'd better go outside!
JOSEPH: Be careful out there!
This is the worst weather I've been out in for a long time.
AMY: Will the boat be OK?
JOSEPH: I hope so. I bought her from an old fisherman—apparently she's been perfectly safe even in the worst weather.
AMY: Where's the *Tampa Queen*, Joseph?
JOSEPH: I don't know. I keep losing her.
AMY: If we've really lost her, we'd better just go home!
JOSEPH: We'll keep looking a little longer.
JESSICA: I've seen her. Look, she's over there.
AMY: Who is?
JESSICA: The *Tampa Queen*. Look.
AMY: Great. Joseph, she's over there. There. Come on!

AMY: Look, there she is. What are those guys doing?
JOSEPH: They're throwing something over the side.
AMY: It's the barrels—the chemicals. This is it. We've got our evidence. Quick, Jessica, get your camera.
JESSICA: OK. But I won't get very good pictures in this weather.
AMY: Come on! When we reach the crests of these waves you get a perfect view—even in these conditions.
JESSICA: OK. I'll do what I can, but don't expect anything special!
AMY: Go on. Go on. Now, before it's too late!

JESSICA: They've seen us. They're turning this way.
AMY: But did you get any good photographs?
JESSICA: Yes, I think I have some really good ones.
JOSEPH: What is the captain of that ship doing? He's heading straight for us.
AMY: He's going to try and sink us. I don't believe it! Get out of his way, Joseph. Get this boat out of the way!
JOSEPH: Oh no! The engine's stopped.
JESSICA: Hurry up. They're getting closer.
JOSEPH: Here, Amy, take the wheel and try to keep her nose into the wind. I'll see if I can fix the engine.
AMY: No, Joseph, here they come.
JESSICA: They're going to smash into us.
AMY: Help!
JOSEPH: Quick, you two. Out on the deck and be ready to jump. It's our only chance.

JOSEPH: Look out—here they come.
AMY: Go away . . . leave us alone!
JESSICA: We're going to die!
JOSEPH: Come on! Jump! Now!
AMY: Help!
JESSICA: Amy, help!

UNIT 17

ANNOUNCER: Acapulco Vacation. A radio drama in nine parts starring Susan Holbrook as Jessica Marley and Courtney Frost as Amy Rosario. Jessica and Amy have gone to sea with Mitch's friend, Joseph. They followed the ship the *Tampa Queen*, but someone saw them and the *Tampa Queen* smashed into Joseph's boat. Jessica, Amy, and Joseph jumped into the water.
Part 8: Missing.

RADIO ANNOUNCER: You're tuned to Radio WQMX, the friendly station. It's four o'clock on a stormy afternoon, so it's Newstime with James Bolton.
BOLTON: Good afternoon. The bad weather in and around the Delta has already claimed several lives. Fears are growing for the safety of two women and their male companion who have been reported missing in a small fishing boat out in the gulf off the coast of Texas.
In the last 24 hours, the coastal regions of the Delta have suffered near-hurricane conditions. Two bridges have been washed away outside Baton Rouge and a 60-year-old man was killed when his car skidded off the highway into the Mississippi. Two boys died in Grand Bayou when they were crushed by a falling tree.
Fears are growing for the safety of two trainee journalists from the *Daily Reporter*. Coast Guard authorities in Galveston say that Jessica Marley and Amy Rosario left the port in a boat belonging to its captain Joseph Baldwin, and they have not been seen since. A sea and air search has been started northwards up the coast but so far there has been no sign of the boat or its crew.
At the United Nations, American ambassador, Michael Bainsberg has again defended the country's attitude . . .

In the newspaper office
ELLIOT: Hi, Frank.
FRANK: You have to stop drinking so much coffee, Bill. That's your fifth cup this morning!
ELLIOT: Thanks for the lecture, Frank. What can I do for you?
FRANK: It's about Jessica and Amy, Bill. I've just had a call from Harvey Freeman.
ELLIOT: Harvey Freeman? I don't follow you. What on earth did he want?
FRANK: He asked me what our reporters were doing on the boat and if we knew what story they were working on.
ELLIOT: What did you say?
FRANK: I told him that we didn't know.
ELLIOT: Yes. Good. But Harvey Freeman??! Maybe the girls were right.

The door opens
MITCH: Mr. Elliot? Bill Elliot, the editor of this newspaper?
ELLIOT: Who are you? And what do you mean coming into my office like this?
MITCH: My name's Mitch Carlton. I'm a friend of your reporters Jessica Marley and Amy Rosario.
ELLIOT: Oh, yes. You're the one they met in Acapulco.
MITCH: Yes, that's right.
ELLIOT: Well, I'm very sorry, Mr. Carlton. I'm afraid we don't have any news. We'll publish a statement as soon as we know anything. Now if you don't mind . . .
MITCH: But you don't understand. I know why your reporters went out in that boat. And I think I know where they are. The Coast Guard is looking in the wrong place.
ELLIOT: What are you talking about?
MITCH: Joseph must have taken them out into the gulf and then south—to see if the *Tampa Queen* was going to throw the chemicals into the sea. But the rescue people have gone north.

ELLIOT:	Well, why don't you tell them what you've just told me?
MITCH:	I tried to. But they won't let me speak to the guy in charge.
ELLIOT:	I see. You know, Mr. Carlton, I think I believe you. Can you tell us where to look?
MITCH:	Yes, I think so.
ELLIOT:	OK. Frank?
FRANK:	Yes?
ELLIOT:	You remember those helicopter people we used on that oil story last month?
FRANK:	Yeah.
ELLIOT:	Get in touch with them again, would you? Ask them if they can give us a chopper and a pilot immediately.
MITCH:	Then you're going to help!
ELLIOT:	Yes, of course. Do you expect me to leave them out there? We've got to find them!

UNIT 18

ANNOUNCER:	Acapulco Vacation. A radio drama in nine parts starring Susan Holbrook as Jessica Marley and Courtney Frost as Amy Rosario. Jessica and Amy have disappeared at sea after their boat was sunk by the *Tampa Queen*. Mitch Carlton has gone to the office of the *Daily Reporter* and has told the editor where he thinks Jessica and Amy are. Part 9: After the Storm.

In a helicopter

ELLIOT:	This is hopeless, Mitch. It'll be dark in another 20 minutes. There's no chance of finding them now.
PILOT:	I'm running low on fuel, Mr. Elliot. We'll have to head back.
ELLIOT:	I'm sorry, Mitch, really I am. OK, let's go.
MITCH:	No! Wait!
ELLIOT:	It's no good, Mitch. Really.
MITCH:	But, Mr. Elliot, look—over there!
ELLIOT:	Where?
MITCH:	Look. Down there. Where I'm pointing. There's something orange in the water. It looks like a life raft.
ELLIOT:	Pilot! Quick. Take us down for a closer look. I think we've found them!
RADIO ANNOUNCER:	You're tuned to Radio WQMX, the friendly station. It's six o'clock, so it's Newstime with James Bolton.
BOLTON:	Good evening. The two reporters missing at sea have been rescued together with their companion. In a

related story, the president of the Dallas company Eastward Chemicals has announced his immediate resignation. We understand that police are investigating chemical dumping at sea by the company and that is why Harvey Freeman is to go.

Jessica Marley and Amy Rosario, two journalists from the *Daily Reporter*, have been rescued from a life raft together with Joseph Baldwin, the man who had taken them out to sea in the boat that sank during Wednesday's gales. They were found by a man who had contacted the editor of their newspaper, the *Daily Reporter*. After their rescue the two women said that they were glad to be alive, and thanked their editor for hiring the helicopter that found them.

Harvey Freeman, the president of Eastward Chemicals, has resigned from the company. A spokesperson for the Houston police department says that Freeman's resignation is connected with the discovery that Eastward Chemicals has been dumping chemical waste into the sea, despite government regulations.

State governor Amanda Pearce, returning from her visit . . .

In the newspaper office

ELLIOT:	Well, I must say I am pleased we found you. I'm sorry I wasn't more helpful at the beginning, but you must understand that the job of a newspaper editor—
AMY:	That's all right, Mr. Elliot—
ELLIOT:	Call me Bill.
AMY:	That's all right . . . uh . . . Bill. Jessica and I are really glad you got that helicopter. If you hadn't found us, we wouldn't have survived.
ELLIOT:	You have a terrible cold there.
AMY:	Yes, I know. Sitting in a life raft in a storm isn't very good for your health!
ELLIOT:	Where's Jessica, by the way?
AMY:	She's talking to Mitch, I think.
ELLIOT:	Well, while we're waiting for her, we might as well have a cup of coffee. Marlene!

Later

MITCH:	Anyway, the Eastward board has asked me to go back to the company. They want me to be the director of their research and development department.
JESSICA:	That's wonderful news.
MITCH:	Has Mr. Elliot forgiven you?
JESSICA:	Gosh, I don't know. Oh no, look at the time! I'm supposed to be with him now. I have to go.
MITCH:	Will I see you again?
JESSICA:	Of course. Just call me. Maybe we could go to Acapulco for a vacation sometime!